On (Writing) Families

On (Writing) Families

Autoethnographies of Presence and Absence, Love and Loss

Edited by

Jonathan Wyatt
The University of Edinburgh, UK

and

Tony E. Adams
Northeastern Illinois University, USA

SENSE PUBLISHERS
ROTTERDAM / BOSTON / TAIPEI

A C.I.P. record for this book is available from the Library of Congress.

ISBN 978-94-6209-620-2 (paperback)
ISBN 978-94-6209-621-9 (hardback)
ISBN 978-94-6209-622-6 (e-book)

Published by: Sense Publishers,
P.O. Box 21858, 3001 AW Rotterdam, The Netherlands
https://www.sensepublishers.com/

Printed on acid-free paper

TABLE OF CONTENTS

TABLE OF CONTENTS

ACKNOWLEDGMENTS

We are grateful to the contributors of this collection—without them, this book would not exist. Their enthusiasm, openness and all-round brilliance have been wonderful to work with. We would also like to thank Tony Colon for his help with editing this manuscript, and to Peter de Liefde for his support as well as the opportunity and honor to publish with Sense Publishers.

Jonathan

I thank the various people around me who have (whether they know it or not) helped sustain me during mine and Tony's work on this book over the past two years. Their contributions to my life, as well as to this collaborative enterprise, are incalculable. Tony gets the first mention. He has to. His consistently cheerful, perceptive, encouraging, smart, efficient presence makes it such a pleasure working with him. (Let's do it again soon, Tony.) Above all, my thanks go to Tessa Wyatt for bearing with this and with me; and to Holly and Joe Wyatt. You make this work meaningful. Really, you do. Finally, I am full of gratitude to my family of origin: Anne, Simon, Nicola, and—my late father—Paul Wyatt. I'm so glad you're there. Here.

Tony

I am grateful to many others for their support of my life and work, especially Brett Aldridge, Mitch Allen, Nilanjana Bardhan, Christopher Birdsong, Derek Bolen, Robin Boylorn, Jay Brower, Marcy Chvasta, Ken Cissna, Norm Denzin, Rachel Dubrofsky, Craig Engstrom, Brian Flowers, Brad Gangnon, Craig Gingrich-Philbrook, Jonny Gray, Andrew Herrmann, Kim Kline, Lenore Langsdorf, Patricia Leavy, Michael LeVan, Jimmie Manning, Michaela Meyer, Nicole Neuman, Mark Neumann, Ron Pelias, Sandy Pensoneau-Conway, Carl Ratner, Jillian Tullis, John Warren, and Jules Wight. I appreciate my students and colleagues at Northeastern Illinois University, including Wilfredo Alvarez, Anna Antaramian, Katrina Bell-Jordan, Bernard Brommel, Rodney Higginbotham, Kristen Hunt, Alan Mace, Nancy McVittie, Cyndi Moran, Seung-Hwan Mun, Shayne Pepper, Nanette Potee, Edie Rubinowitz, and Angie Sweigart-Gallagher. I would also like to thank Stacy Holman Jones for her motivation and loving ability to cultivate my writing-self, Keith Berry for informing every facet of my life, Art Bochner for teaching me about love, fatherhood, and family life, and Carolyn Ellis for the courage to reframe my past (her mentorship inspired "Ties that Bind, Ties that Scar," the concluding chapter of this collection). I thank my stepfather, Michael Rome, and my parents, Phil Adams and Sheri Rome, for their dedication and support especially when I am distant and cantankerous, and I thank Jonathan Wyatt for joining me on this book-editing adventure—if you can tolerate me again, I look forward to our next project. And, of course, I thank Gerardo (Jerry) Moreno for loving me through many days and nights of breathing, reading, writing, and editing.

JONATHAN WYATT AND TONY E. ADAMS

INTRODUCTION

I (Jonathan) am writing time away. Café Lucano, on Edinburgh's George IV Bridge, serves excellent coffee and the servers are patient with me. At a nearby table, visitors to the city talk about plans for the day. A few people sit alone reading, writing, or playing with their smart phones. One man, in his mid-thirties, watches traffic pass. He is still, unhurried, content.

A bell rings at the hatch to my left and the server approaches, comments to the chef in Italian, laughs, collects breakfasts, and carries them past me—the bacon roll smells good—to a young woman and her mother.

In three weeks, my eighty-something mother will visit us from her home in Godalming, a town southwest of London, as long as the infection she is fighting is defeated. It will be her first and probably only visit: soon, she says, she will not feel up to it. She will fly. I will collect her and deliver her to the homely hotel we've found in the New Town district and, from there, we will have the weekend to introduce her to the city's historical delights. She does not walk far these days so we will wheel her up and down Edinburgh's plentiful, unforgiving hills. She will not be able to climb the stairs to our rented third floor flat, though she is determined that she will.

We will seek out restaurants that serve the plain food she can eat, find drives that she will enjoy, and plan a schedule flexible enough to take account of her varying energy patterns. Perhaps, as we sit wrapped up by the beach at Portobello, we will talk about my father and wonder if he would have swum in the bracing water. At the end of the weekend, she will fly home and I will again worry that it was unkind of me to move us so far away. And I will speculate about what she feels but does not say.

*

I imagine Tony sitting with me. I wish he were here, differently present. We could pore over these beautiful chapters together, be at this table with this book, whose title we have now settled on: *On (Writing) Families: Autoethnographies of Presence and Absence, Love and Loss*.[1]

Tony and I met at the annual International Congress of Qualitative Inquiry in Urbana-Champaign, USA, in 2007, soon after I had read Tony's poignant writing about his father (Adams, 2006). Our contact that year spawned a series of annual panels on sons and fathers at the conference as well as "On (Writing) Fathers," a special issue of *Qualitative Inquiry* devoted to father-son writings (Wyatt & Adams, 2012). The collection contributed to our understanding of father-son

J. Wyatt & T. E. Adams (eds.), On (Writing) Families, 1 6.

relationships as well as the ways in which "fathers accompany us through our lives" (p. 119).

However, while we focused on father-son writings, we missed many other relationships. "Where are the daughters?" one person asked. "Do any of the writers say anything about mothers?" asked another. We then arrived at this book—a sequel of sorts—that included a variety of relational accounts. We do include a few more stories of fathers and sons (Bolen; Gingrich-Philbrook; Herrmann; Mather), but also stories of fathers and daughters (Boylorn; Rowe; Holman Jones; Speedy), mothers and sons (Freeman), daughters and mothers (Allegranti; Douglas; Harris; Leavy), and more comprehensive accounts of parents, children, and familial experience (Bondi; Jonsdottir; Tamas; Wright). Throughout, contributors complicate what family means and how families are lived and, like the father-son journal issue, illustrate the ways in which our roles as parents, as children, and as family members "remain meaningful, both through and beyond life" (Wyatt & Adams, 2012, p. 119).

*

Last weekend I walked amongst the Pentland Hills, just south of Edinburgh. My route took me first to an ancient fort, which, to my untrained eye, seemed a series of attractive grass mounds. From there I wandered along the stone road that skirted an army firing range covered in barbed wire and hectoring red-letter warnings. Relieved to leave this area, I strayed from the undulating track to join a steep path towards a minor peak. Shifting from the certainty of compacted stones onto the intricate doubt of a weaving trail through rocks, moss, and earth, I found myself walking into and with the stories in this collection.

After some minutes, I paused to catch my breath; the climb felt steep and I'm out of hill-walking practice. I looked west to where the hills stretched towards Glasgow, and I felt immersed in these essays' sense of place and how each takes the reader into the sensuality of presence. I could picture the home where Mark Freeman visits his mother, its dayroom where he sits beside her slumped figure, seeking to make contact. I sensed the dust—which I imagined to be red—thrown into the air, and then to the ground, and then to the air again, of Mort Mather's father's departing jeep. I was in the garage of Derek Bolen's house, surrounded by his father's work-in-progress. I became full of his father in that space, and awash with sadness that he was not as present as Derek wanted him to be. I was with Jeannie Wright arguing with her father, inhaling his cigarette smoke, seeing him in dreams. I rode in Patricia Leavy's car with her daughter, listening to Katy Perry, and I found myself on the steps of Robin Boylorn's childhood home, searching for her father, willing him into view.

(These days, more than I have for years, I search for my father in Edinburgh. I glimpse him in the gait of a limping man, in a shock of white hair through planes of shop glass, his flown laugh reaching me from the corner of a room. Edinburgh and our top floor flat is my first home that he never knew.)

Recovered, I pressed on and up. A man on a bike, jolting tentatively down the slope, passed me without greeting, then a friendlier walker, for whose smile I was grateful. At the cliff top I looked northeast over Edinburgh's suburbs and the crags of Arthur's Seat. There, in that glimpse, were the settings of these stories: Jane Speedy, lying on a cliff, cracking the crossword with her dad; the stoop of Anne Harris' mother's house where Harris waits and waits and waits; watching Beatrice Allegranti performing capoeira, her mother looking on; the dream-sharing kitchens of Gunnhildur Una Jonsdottir's stories of her mother and daughter; the kitchen table at which Stacy Holman Jones read the phone book aloud to her dad; and the haunting presence of Liz Bondi's father's homeland. Pausing on and atop that Edinburgh hillside, I was in each of these places; they were—and they remain—in me. The spatial, writes Massey (2005), enables "new relations-to-each-other of previously disparate trajectories" (p. 41).

As I made a quarter-turn to my left, I could identify Fife across the seemingly still waters of the Firth of Forth. The Pentlands, on which I stood, are small hills, but after twenty-five years of Oxford's relative plane, I felt on top of the world.

*

The chapters in this collection call me to bring "the person I think of loosely as 'me'"—to use Craig Gingrich-Philbrook's exquisite phrase—to this page. They find a way inside me; they call me; they invite me to make connections. The chapters show me what parents, children, and families can mean, not in any sentimental sense, but rather how they matter even if we wish that they didn't. The chapters respond to Della Pollock's (2009) call for the creative work of "writing, critique, and embodiment, conjoined in the possibility of making a different history, of making our most intimate histories differently" (p. 646), and they illustrate how family stories can orient us to "identity, a sense of place, and the meaning of life" (Sterk & Deakins, 2012, p. xiii).

My awareness of their palpable sense of place prompts me to consider these chapters' crafting—their art. I am struck by variations in style and form: how textual distinctions carry the narratives differently, how authors write from various perspectives, how one author offers a chapter in "fragments"—short, snapshot sections that speak perhaps of stuttering, hesitant relating and that show writing's provisionality—and another who takes a more direct narrative line. Sophie Tamas writes in the present tense in numbered sections that provide peeks—some brief, some longer—into her experience: a phone conversation with her mother, tending to her ailing grandfather, supper with her parents, her eldest child returning home. Kitrina Douglas offers an extended narrative, in the here-and-now, of a crisis in her past professional sporting career and her mother's part in supporting her through leaving this career; she follows the account with theoretical reflections on how we might understand the experience. Desirée Rowe dwells retrospectively on the meanings of her father's tattoo, a photograph of which hangs in her office; her writing is almost a meditation. Mort Mather's stories of his relationship with his father provide an affecting, gentle sequence of narratives that shift between early childhood, young adulthood, and now, and Jane Speedy moves between vivid, touching stories, tinted with humour, of her father's last illness and tales of her early memories of being with him.

Hence, too, the authors work differently with time. Some take us back and forth between now and then: Craig Gingrich-Philbrook begins with an uneasy here-and-now experience before, as a knowing narrator, taking us back to where the experience began. Derek Bolen holds us steady alongside him as he explains his experiences and then bears us into the immediacy of past moments and episodes. Liz Bondi and Robin Boylorn move between the past and the present tense, taking us close to experience then drawing us back. These authors take us with them on journeys between "what happened" and "how it is now." Others, like Rowe and Freeman, in a sense stand still, showing us "there and then" retrospectively, or, like Tamas, carry us with them through the continuous present, the past being glimpsed through the interactions of the here and now, family histories passed, casually, between writer and reader.

"Narrative," Mark Freeman (1998) has written elsewhere, "grows out of the very temporal conditions of our existence" (p. 47), and these essays, inevitably perhaps in a book about family relationships, foreground our temporality and mortality: what can and cannot be hoped for in our remaining (physical) time together, what can and cannot be regretted or forgiven, what is lost or has never been found or will never be. Beatrice Allegranti ponders the "temporal mourning" of her late mother's birthday, moving between addressing her mother ("I dreamt of you last night") and writing obliquely of her mother's history and its link with her own: "We carry our ancestral, genetic line, other bodies, others' stories, in our body." Jonsdottir crafts tender accounts of illness and vulnerability, both hers and across generations, and of how hands reach out to help. Andrew Herrmann wonders about "living [his] father's unfinished narrative"; his father is probably alive, yet unknown and out-of-touch. Wright offers us the rawness of her recent loss, viewed through the prism of her attachment to—and the politics of—a treasured artefact.

All of the authors also make great play of the presence-absence dialectic: presence, as indicated by attention to and time with others (Bolen; Douglas; Leavy; Tamas), acknowledgment and recognition (Freeman), being bound by/to genetics and biology (Allegranti; Harris; Herrmann), and by shared experiences, memories, and artifacts (Bondi; Rowe; Wright); absence, as indicated by leaving, dying, and disappearing (Boylorn; Herrmann; Harris; Mather; Speedy), of failing bodies (Freeman; Holman Jones), of being physically apart, separated by distance (Tamas), and of nonexistent genetic connections that cultivate and perpetuate erroneous assumptions and expectations of kinship and commitment (Allegranti; Harris; Herrmann). Presence and absence entangled, informing our biological and social experiences of/as families as well as about what family is (not) and how we should (not) be together.

Inseparable from and layered with the presence-absence dialectic is the interaction between love and loss. As evidenced in many of the essays, there is a sense of wanting to be present, a being with constitutive of love; as Allegranti aptly notes, "It's the everyday being-together activities that make up a life, and a loving-in-action" (also see Douglas). There is love, marked by infatuation and dedication, of wanting to be so very close but a love simultaneously constituted by loss, marked by struggles and stumbles in talk, touch, and time spent together. There is love, indicated by commitment, and loss, indicated by confusion about who parents, children, and families are, or have ever been (Boylorn; Herrmann; Rowe). At times, reciprocated and unconditional love shines (Bolen; Bondi; Douglas; Freeman; Leavy); at other times, this love quickly turns to loss, to conditional exchanges and refusals of recognition (Allegranti; Harris; Herrmann). Love, marked by respect, of saying or writing to family members (Speedy); loss, marked by what a person could not say because of fear or circumstance (Bolen; Jonsdottir; Mather). Love, in moments of bliss and content, and loss in longing for unachievable certainties and truths (Bondi; Herrmann), in mourning the failures and inadequacies of others (Boylorn; Harris), in missing previous, absent versions of parents (Freeman; Holman Jones; Wright), and in wishes that the conditions of families could have been otherwise.

*

What I've written here feels both too much and too little. Too much, in that I worry that I've given away more about the chapters than I should; too little because there's so much more to tell about this collection's delights. Perhaps such doubt is part of this introduction-writing process. I'll just add some final exhortations then, before I gather my belongings, return to the office, and write to Tony: Savor the essays, one-by-one. Absorb them, live with them. Walk hills with them. Drink with them in busy cafés as you gaze at the traffic or eat bacon rolls. See what they call forth in and from you.

NOTES

[1] Autoethnography is a research method that uses personal experience to describe—and sometimes critique—cultural beliefs, experiences, and practices. Autoethnographers engage in laborious and nuanced self-reflection—typically referred to as "reflexivity"—in order to identify and interrogate the intersections between self and society and to show "people in the process of figuring out what to do, how to live, and the meaning of their struggles" (Bochner & Ellis, 2006, p. 111). Autoethnographers try to balance methodological rigor, emotion, and creativity, and they write with an attention toward improving personal/social life. For comprehensive accounts of autoethnography, see Adams, Holman Jones, and Ellis (forthcoming), Ellis (2004, 2009), Ellis, Adams, and Bochner (2011), Ellis and Bochner (2000), Holman Jones (2005), Holman Jones, Adams, and Ellis (2013), Muncey (2010), Poulos (2013), Short, Turner, and Grant (2013), and Sikes (2013).

In this collection, writers use autoethnography to describe—and sometimes critique—their experiences as parents, children, and families. They use creativity, emotion, and rigorous reflexivity in order to show their processes of "figuring out what to do, how to live, and the meaning of their [familial] struggles" (Bochner & Ellis, 2006, p. 111).

REFERENCES

Adams, T. E. (2006). Seeking father: Relationally reframing a troubled love story. *Qualitative Inquiry*, *12*, 704-723.

Adams, T. E., Holman Jones, S., & Ellis, C. (forthcoming). *Autoethnography*. Oxford: Oxford University Press.

Bochner, A. P., & Ellis, C. S. (2006). Communication as autoethnography. In G. J. Shepherd, J. St. John, & T. Striphas (Eds.), *Communication as ... Perspectives on theory* (pp. 110-122). Thousand Oaks, CA: Sage.

Ellis, C. (2004). *The ethnographic I: A methodological novel about autoethnography*. Walnut Creek, CA: AltaMira Press.

Ellis, C. (2009). *Revision: Autoethnographic reflections on life and work*. Walnut Creek, CA: Left Coast Press.

Ellis, C., Adams T. E., & Bochner, A. P. (2011). Autoethnography: An overview. *Forum: Qualitative Social Research, 12*(1). Retrieved from http://www.qualitative-research.net/index.php/fqs/article/view/1589/3095

Ellis, C., & Bochner, A. P. (2000). Autoethnography, personal narrative, reflexivity. In N. K. Denzin & Y. S. Lincoln (Eds.), *Handbook of qualitative research* (2nd ed., pp. 733-768). Thousand Oaks, CA: Sage.

Freeman, M. (1998). Mythical time, historical time and the narrative fabric of the self. *Narrative Inquiry, 8*, 27-50.

Holman Jones, S. (2005). Autoethnography: Making the personal political. In N. K. Denzin & Y. S. Lincoln (Eds.), *Handbook of qualitative research* (3rd ed., pp. 763-791). Thousand Oaks, CA: Sage.

Holman Jones, S., Adams, T. E., & Ellis, C. (Eds.). (2013). *Handbook of autoethnography*, Walnut Creek, CA: Left Coast Press.

Massey, D. (2005). *For space*. London: Sage.

Muncey, T. (2010). *Creating autoethnographies*. Thousand Oaks, CA: Sage.

Pollock, D. (2009). Beyond experience. *Cultural Studies ⇔ Critical Methodologies, 9*, 636-646.

Poulos, C. N. (2013). Autoethnography. In A. A. Trainor & E. Graue (Eds.), *Reviewing qualitative research in the social sciences* (pp. 38-53). New York: Routledge.

Short, N. P., Turner, L., & Grant A. (Eds.). (2013). *Contemporary British autoethnography*. Rotterdam, the Netherlands: Sense Publishers.

Sikes, P. (Ed.). (2013). *Autoethnography*. Thousand Oaks, CA: Sage.

Sterk, H. M. & Deakins, A. H. (2011). Introduction. In A. H. Deakins, R. B. Lockridge, & H. M. Sterk (Eds.), *Mothers and daughters: Complicated connections across cultures* (pp. xiii-xxv). Lanham, MD: University Press of America.

Wyatt. J., & Adams, T. E. (Eds.) (2012a). Special issue: On (writing) fathers. *Qualitative Inquiry, 18*, 119-209.

Wyatt. J., & Adams, T. E. (2012b). Introduction: On (writing) fathers. *Qualitative Inquiry, 18*, 119-120.

Jonathan Wyatt
Counselling and Psychotherapy
The University of Edinburgh

Tony E. Adams
Department of Communication, Media and Theatre
Northeastern Illinois University

MORT MATHER

FATHERLY LOVE

AT THIRTEEN

Dad left today. Cubby and I watched him check the oil and water in the jeep which he does just about every time before he leaves for anywhere. When he was done, he put his hand on my shoulder and said, "Well son, this is it; I'm on my way. Take care of your mother. Be good." Then he got into the jeep.

The jeep started right up. It always did. He takes good care of it and knows how to fix anything that goes wrong. The jeep turned right out of the yard. Cubby and I watched it go past the barn and the cherry trees starting to kick up dust but there was no dust as he passed the Webber's because the road truck puts down oil on the road in front of houses when the road gets dry and dusty. After it passed the Webber's the jeep started to kick up dust again an' then, as it went down hill, it was like it was sinking into the earth until all we could see was the dust. We just stood there watching until we couldn't hear the motor anymore and the dust settled and then we stood there some more. I guess I kept thinking that he would come back. I didn't cry or anything. After a while I got some stones and sat on the bank an' threw them across the road at a tree. I'm not a good thrower so I didn't hit the tree very often.

Then Mom came out of the house and sat down next to me and put her arm around me and we both just sat and then she asked me if I wanted a piece of pie. Now there's a dumb question; she's a super pie maker and I knew it would be a cherry pie because I picked the cherries.

EARLIER THAT YEAR

It was raining the day Dad told me he was leaving. We were hanging out in the wagon shed. I was sorting out nuts an' bolts an' washers of which there are lots that were there when we first moved to the farm when I was five. They are in cans mostly, coffee cans and tobacco cans, lined up on a beam on the wall and I guess people just put them in the cans to have them handy when they needed a bolt for something though they weren't new. Some were rusty and some were greasy but there weren't any bent ones or ones with messed up threads. I use them whenever I need to. I made a cart out of some scraps of wood and some wheels that came off of something and the bolts came in handy for doing that, especially the U-bolts, and I had one bolt that went down through the center of the riding board and into the center of the board that I attached the front wheels to with two U-bolts. I put the bolt through a couple of washers between the two boards and I could sit on the

J. Wyatt & T. E. Adams (eds.), On (Writing) Families, 7–11.
© *2014 Sense Publishers. All rights reserved.*

riding board with my feet on the steering board and make it go in the direction I wanted.

Dad was changing the oil in the jeep. He was always very careful to get the top of the oil can clean before he pushed in the spout. He said dirt was the biggest enemy of an engine. You see, the pistons move up and down in the engine in like a tunnel only really tight and the oil keeps the pistons from rubbing on the tunnels but if the oil is dirty instead of being smooth it's like sandpaper and it wears out the pistons and then the oil gets into the combustion chamber and burns and that's why some cars and trucks have a lot of smoke coming out of their exhaust pipes.

When he was done he stood in the door of the wagon shed looking out at the rain and wiping his hands with a rag. It wasn't raining very hard but it was kinda chilly so you wouldn't want ta actually do anything outside. I went and stood beside him and he told me he was going West and never coming back East. Well, I thought that was OK because I liked it out West with the mountains and waterfalls and all but then he said that I wasn't coming with him; that I was to stay with my mother, he said. I asked him why Mom wasn't going West and he said he didn't love her anymore and just then Mom came running out of the house screaming and crying and saying "Don't! Oh, please don't." And she saw us and she just fell down in the wet grass and was sobbing; and then I saw that I was crying too. I didn't even know it. And Dad just stood there and so did I. I didn't know what to do. And then Mom got up and went back into the house.

I turned my face away so Dad wouldn't see I was crying and I wiped my face with my sleeve. I kinda expected Dad to put his hand on my shoulder or something but he didn't. He just stood there. Cubby was there sitting beside me and I went down and hugged him and that felt good.

I stood up and brushed off my knees and we stood there some more and then I asked him why I couldn't go with him and he said he didn't love me anymore either and my eyes started to get wet again so I just kicked him and ran into the house.

Mom was sitting at the kitchen table with her head resting on her arms. She looked up when she heard the door bang and her eyes and nose were all red and she turned on the chair and held out her arms. I ran to her and we held each other and she kept saying, "I'm sorry" over and over and hugging me. I was sorry too but I wasn't sure what I was sorry about.

FIVE YEARS LATER

The bus slowed at midnight, the time the bus was due in Jacob Lake. I picked up my bag with the clothes I would wear for the next couple of months and moved to the front. It was dark everywhere except for the headlights; no house lights, no cars or trucks, just the road. Then the headlights picked up a building with a gas pump out front and then the sign on the building "Jacob Lake Trading Post" and then I saw the jeep. Dad got out of the jeep and came toward me as the bus pulled away.

"You've grown quite a bit," he said as he took my bag.

"Yep. I guess." What else should I say? So have you? You look good? How are you doing? We got in the jeep and he congratulated me on graduating from high school and asked how my trip had been. I told him about the plane ride to Chicago and the bus to Flagstaff and spending the day walking around Flagstaff until the bus to Salt Lake City left. It all seemed quite boring. He told me it would take about an hour on this dirt road before we came to the turn off for the fire lookout tower he manned and where he lived all summer until the first snow.

We didn't really have much to say. It was awkward.

My mind was churning around my desire to get my parents back together. I blurted, "I think Mom still loves you." I hadn't intended to say that so soon, maybe not at all but he wasn't saying anything. He seemed to savor that but then he told me I had a brother and sister.

A brother and a sister? The headlights bounced along the road ahead and reflected off the trees close by both sides. The letters I'd gotten over the past five years; not that many but still; a brother and a sister? How did that happen? Well, I know how it happens but …

"Does Grandma know?" I visited my grandmother and grandfather several times a year. Usually my mother and I drove down to Philadelphia for the day and once a year I would take the bus and stay for several days, time spent mostly reading the funny papers my grandmother saved for me all year long. Dad was their only child, born nine months after they were married, and, it seemed, the focus of the rest of my grandmother's life.

"No. No one back East knows. You can spread the word or not as you wish."

It turns out his passion for painting western landscapes was not the only reason he left the East. He left my mother and me and the East for another woman, someone he worked with in New York. When he drove away five years ago he headed for the train station before turning west. My half brother was three and my half sister eighteen months.

When the first snow came to the Kaibab Forest the tower was closed until fire danger returned next year. Five of us, Dad driving, his second wife, Betty and I squeezed into the passenger seat and half-brother Davy and half-sister Lisa tucked into cracks and crevasses in the load behind the seats. We were headed for San Francisco where I would catch a plane back East and join the Coast Guard for four years; my father would check in with a gallery that was handling his paintings in the hope there would be some money for them. It was a scenic trip including Bryce, Zion National Park where we spent more than a week hiking, Death Valley, Mt. Whitney and Lake Tahoe.

EIGHT YEARS LATER

On my last Easter break before graduating from the University of Wisconsin I took another trip to see my father. A friend and I headed for Oak Creek Canyon south of Flagstaff where he was staying for the winter. My half-brother Davy was now eleven and he had four sisters, the last two were twins. No surprises this time as I had been kept up to date with letters, artwork and pictures from my half-siblings and their mother. My friend Jay, Davy, my father and I hiked into the Grand Canyon for four days. Jay and my father hit it off wonderfully talking philosophy whenever they had an opportunity. Jay wrote with a brown pen because nothing was black and white. Argh. On the third day we were sprawled out recuperating from a strenuous morning in a shelter where the Bright Angel Trail starts snaking up from the river to a campground on the tonto—a broad platform between the inner gorge and the rest of the colorful canyon walls. We had finished lunch when something set me off. I grabbed my pack and headed up the trail alone. Bullshit, bullshit, bullshit, enough, more than enough bullshit, enough to last a lifetime and then, suddenly, I was no longer tired, the pack on my back more like wings than weight. I spun around in the trail taking pictures of the incredible beauty all around me. The hike was all up hill but I felt no gravitational pull. I was as close to flying as I will likely ever be. When I got to the campground I dropped my pack on the first picnic table and headed out onto the tonto, a 3-mile trail taking me to the edge of the inner gorge. I had only one frame left in my camera which I reserved for the sunset. When I got back to the campground dinner was ready. I was hungry but overwhelmingly filled with joy. I seriously considered a round trip to the canyon rim that night to get film. Was my joy some sort of bonding with the magnificent Canyon or severing a bond with my father? No matter!

ANOTHER FIVE YEARS

At 32 my stage managing career was going well. I had visited my father in Big Sur, California a couple of years before. Now I was in California again with my bride hoping to hook up with him so they could meet.

The VW bug had served us well getting around Los Angeles. I had hired Barbara as wardrobe mistress for live performances of the *Play of Daniel* and the *Play of Herod* with New York Pro Musica. Job over, we started our honeymoon. We were headed for Paradise; that is General Delivery, Paradise, Arizona, the last address I had for my father. I had written that I would come to him wherever he was and I asked him for directions. Receiving none I called my Grandmother but she didn't have more up-to-date information. The postmaster directed us to a house where he thought they might have been but he suspected they had left though they left no forwarding address.

Released from the mission of trying to introduce my wife to my father we set off exploring the beauty of the southwest which included passing through Zion where we spent a day. Barbara and I hiked in to Emerald Pools and on the return loop came to the Lady Mountain trail head, an amazing trail I had hiked with my stepmother fourteen years ago. Barbara went back to the car while I climbed fast to get as high as possible before it got too dark for a safe return. When I opened a log book part way up the trail my heart gave a leap. The last people to hike this trail, four months before, were my father and five half-siblings.

*

Nearly two years later my father and wife met for the first and last time when we learned that my stepmother had died of cancer in Minnesota where her family lived; that on her death bed she told her family to get the children away from my father; and that he had kidnapped one of them and taken off with all five feeling that he was a fugitive. We also learned that while we were looking for them in Paradise they were in Mexico and that Davy and one of the twins had been taken by riptide and drowned. The bodies were never found.

We caught up with my father and three half-sisters in Big Spring, Arkansas and lived in their tent village for a couple of days. We learned that Davy had been communicating with a friend of the family regularly until his death and my father had sent a last "letter" to this friend in Davy's handwriting, a fiction piece Davy had written about going to Planet X, the idea conveyed being that Davy was going to Planet X and would not be heard from again.

I expressed concern that this person should be allowed to know the fate of a family he had been close to for many years (he had been around most of the times I visited). I convinced my father to give me Bob's address and I assured him I would not reveal the family's whereabouts. I wrote to Bob using the address given. He never responded. Instead I got a letter from my father telling me that he had gone to Planet X.

I exploded with every expletive I had become adept at using while in the service. "That's it, I'm done with you." Yeah, well, that's the old "you can't fire me, I quit" routine but when I told my mother this story with perhaps a few expletives deleted she told me that the only time she and my father fought was when he told her he was going to tell me he was leaving because he didn't love me anymore.

*

Recollections can be dicey. I have in more recent times questioned if I really kicked my father. I do believe my mother's recollection, however I give her tremendous credit for never having a bad word for my father until I unleashed all the anger that might have been pent up in her all those years.

That was the last time I saw my father. There were times when I mused about what I would do if he turned up at my door needing help. I never came across an answer. I'm glad I never had to.

Barbara and I were watching a television movie of a son working for his father in construction. The father was harder on his son than on any of his other workers to the extent the other workers tried to get him to ease up but he loved his son and was just putting him through fire to make him stronger. In the end they hugged and I sobbed uncontrollably for several minutes. Barbara held me as I tried to bring myself under control and finally I choked out, "All I wanted was a hug."

Mort Mather
Organic Farmer/Independent Scholar

11

STACY HOLMAN JONES

ALWAYS STRANGE

Transforming Loss

It's not as if an "I" exists independently over here and then simply loses a "you" over there, especially if the attachment to "you" is part of what composes who "I" am … I have lost "you" only to discover that "I" have gone missing as well.

—Judith Butler, *Precarious Life* (2004, p. 22)

She seemed utterly alone, the silence and darkness impenetrable forever. She fought down panic until she heard her father's voice coming to her very faintly.

—Madeline L'Engle, *A Wrinkle in Time* (1962, p. 167)

WHAT MATTERS

She had been so certain that the moment she found her father everything would be all right. Everything would be settled.[1]

My father and I are watching college football. Well, he is watching college football and I am reading and keeping an eye on the television. Every now and again I ask a question, trying to keep myself in the game.

We are sitting in the living room of the house I am renovating from just this side of wrecked, just this side of despair.

We are sitting in the living room of the only house I could afford in the neighborhood where my old house—the house I shared with my now ex-husband and daughter—sits. I am renovating this house, my house, so that my daughter and I might start a new life that resembles, however modestly, the old one.

My father is here to help me with the renovation. On the few occasions he has visited me without my mother along, he has come to work: on the kitchen, on the yard, on the windows, on the porch. And today, as we take a break from our renovation of my life, I want to talk. I want to ask him something, but I am afraid.

"Dad," I begin, feeling clumsy but determined. "We've not talked about me being gay. I feel like we should … What do you think about it?"

My heart is pounding. Why is it so hard to get the words out? I watch him. He studies the screen.

J. Wyatt & T. E. Adams (eds.), On (Writing) Families, 13–21.

"I don't understand it," he begins, his eyes fixed on the blur of grass and uniforms. "I don't think it's right. But it's your decision and I want you to be happy."

"I *am* happy, Dad."

"That's all that matters."

I wait, but he doesn't speak. I try again. "Is there anything else you want to say?"

"No. As long as you're happy, your mother and I are happy."

Not wanting to push him, but also not wanting this stiff discomfort, I say, "Okay. I'm glad to know that. But if there's ever anything else, or if you want to talk some more ...."

Halftime begins and my father changes the channel, looking for another game.

I return to the book lying open in my hands, to my racing mind and beating heart, to my self, looking for another chance, another choice.[2] I feel the chasm deepen between us, feel our relationship unraveling as we retreat into ourselves. Though who am I without him? My ability to *be* implicates my father in me. My own foreignness to myself is the source of my connection to him. I cannot know or understand myself—fully, or ever—because who I am includes traces of him.[3] Traces of mis-understanding, mis-recognition. Traces of protection and dismissal.[4] Traces of *not right*. My confession[5]—the words "I am gay" as a manifestation of my desires, my choices, my self—puts me at risk of losing him.[6] Of losing what it is in my father, what it is in me, that I cannot reach, know, or name.

DEPENDS ON WHO YOU ASK

There was no question, despite the change in him, that he was her father.[7]

Since my father visited me in Tampa, I have been afraid to see him, afraid to talk with him. After that visit—after my failed attempt to talk with my father about my sexuality, my choices, my self—everything changed. *He* changed. He had another heart attack (his third) and needed open heart surgery (his second). And then he had a stroke in the recovery room after surgery. A *stroke* a year after he'd been in Tampa, strong and sure, helping me renovate my house and my life. A stroke and then the emergency surgery to repair a perforated bowel, the fall in rehab, the colostomy bag, the partially paralyzed left arm and leg, the emptiness in his eyes and speech.

*

He'd emerged from open-heart surgery groggy and testy. He'd grumbled that he felt like a horse was sitting on his chest. But he was alive and the surgery to clear the blocked artery had been a success. My mother, relieved and exhausted, went home to feed the dogs. I stayed behind so I could see my father during the last 10-minute visiting session permitted until morning. I returned to my perch in the bone-aching cold of the waiting room, though just a few minutes into my wait, the intensive care nurse approached. "Can I sneak in early?" I asked hopefully.

"In a bit, yes. I'm afraid, though, that there's been a change in your father's condition."

"What do you mean? He was just awake, and complaining."

"He's had a stroke. I'm not sure how significant. They're going to take him downstairs for some tests."

The panicked feeling I'd carried all day flooded my body anew. "Can I see him?"

"Yes, but only for a minute."

*

I walk into the room and my father's eyes open. He gives me a lop-sided smile that turns into a grimace.

"You okay?"

He raises his right hand and makes the motion of writing. I retrieve the pen and small pad from the bedside table. I put the pen in his hand and rest the paper on the bed. Dad writes, "Chest crushed. Hard to breathe." Two nurses enter the room. "We're going to take your Dad downstairs now. You can see him in the morning when visiting hours resume at nine. We'll take good care of him."

I take the pen and paper from my father and squeeze his hand. The nurses push the bed toward the door, then bang it hard against the door frame. "Please be careful with him!" I call out. "Dad, don't worry. I'll see you soon." I stand alone in the room, machines blinking silently around me. Chest crushed, hard to breathe. I lift the receiver of the bedside phone and wait for my mother's voice on the other end of the line.

*

I stay with my father in the hospital for several days. There's a clear and sure line that demarcates my father before and after the stroke. Before: active, opinionated, capable, kind, a caretaker, body in the grip of unrelenting heart disease. After: dependent, depressed, unable to use his left arm or leg, forgetful in the immediate but a keen memory of the past, mind unsure of the structure and strictures of time, language, and talk.[8] My bedside vigil had to end, though. I needed to return home to my daughter and my work. I call my mother every day to talk about my father, until she tells me that my calls aren't necessary. "There's just nothing new to tell you," she says.

Once my father is released from the hospital and sent home, I call him—every few days at first, then every few weeks, then less. Our brief and stilted conversations center on how he's feeling and his rehabilitation, though occasionally our exchanges turn to other things. My father's talk is uncensored;[9] he says whatever comes into his mind. Sometimes his talk is funny, as when he needles my mother about her repeated promises that "dinner will be ready in 15 minutes." Sometimes his talk is openly emotional, as when he tells me how much he loves the new puppy my mother brought home. Sometimes his talk is disarming and cutting, as when he informs me that a boy I went to high school with has died. While I express my shock and sadness, I can hear my mother correcting my father in the background. "What?" Dad says to her. "Oh."

"Nevermind," he says to me.

"Nevermind what?"

"Mom says Sam didn't die. He's *gay*."

I exhale. "Oh. That's a relief."

Dad says, "Depends on who you ask."

I don't say anything.

I don't say what I am thinking: Who counts as human? Whose lives count *as lives*? What makes for a grievable life?[10]

And my father doesn't say what he is thinking, either. What counts as a loss of life? What counts as a loss of self? He is still alive, still an aging and ill white man, still my father. I am still alive, still—now, though not always—gay, still his daughter. We have both experienced a radical shift in the flow of our identities;[11] we may wish to recreate our selves as if we were there all along,[12] though to do so we must be fully human to one another. Our losses and grief must *count*—to ourselves, to each other, and to the world. Though the kinds of losses—of people and selves and relationships—that we can acknowledge and avow as loss *depend*. They depend on who you ask. After all, if someone is lost, and that person is not someone (or some*body*), then what and where is the loss, and how does mourning take place?[13]

ALWAYS STRANGE

She realized with a flooding horror that she could see him ... but her father could not ... see her. She looked at him in panic, his eyes were the same steady blue that she remembered.[14]

During another phone conversation, my father asks how my daughter and I like living in the renovated house. I tell him, "We're getting used to it," and my father says, "Does the baby know you're a queer?" using a word his grandmother—my great grandmother—and not he, at least not before the stroke—would have used.

"Yes, Dad. The *baby* is seven and she knows I'm gay."

"You can't be a *gay*. You were married for 15 years for christsakes."

"Twelve."

"Twelve what?"

"I was married for twelve ... never mind. Yes, the baby knows I'm gay," I say, then revise. "Knows I'm queer."

"Gay. Queer. Whatever you call yourselves these days. Your mother and I should have known."

"Should have known what?"

"Should have known about you."

"How could you have known? I didn't know—who or what I am, who or what I love. I still don't."

"Well, we knew one thing."

"What's that?"

"We knew you were strange. *You* were always strange."

"And what would *you* know about being strange?"

My father laughs. "A hellava lot. All these braces and bags and metal? You should see me. I look like a monster."

"Thank goodness you are a lovable monster."

My father doesn't say anything. And I don't say what I am thinking: that since the change, since the shifts in our identities and our relationship, we have been asking each other to see us for who and what we are, as we always have been, as we were, *before*.[15] Though I am trying to know that when we ask for this kind of recognition, we petition the future *in relation* to each other.[16] In the asking, familiar stories become strange and we rewrite our losses.[17] In the asking, we instigate a transformation, having already become something new.[18]

A WRINKLE IN TIME

Don't be afraid to be afraid ... That is all we can do.[19]

I visit my parents in the stifling July heat. I haven't been home in a while. During the visit, my father makes a series of attempts to connect with my 10-year-old daughter. He finds a beach volleyball game on television and they watch together. He asks if she plays beach volleyball. He asks if she can spike the ball. He asks if she dives into the sand. She says, "Yes" and "Sometimes" and "Of course." Each time she answers, my daughter looks away from the game and over at my father. She holds his gaze for only a moment, then shifts her eyes back to the set.

My father isn't watching the game. He is watching her. His questioning stops, though his gaze remains fixed, steady. After several moments, my daughter looks up from the game and over at my father. She gets up from the couch and moves to stand next to my father's recliner. She shifts her hip and leg up onto the armrest and leans her weight into my father's shoulder. He pats her knee with his braced left hand. He lets his eyes settle on the blur of sand and uniforms.

Later that evening, I ask my mother if Dad is still reading. While reading was a struggle, my father had kept at it, unable to give up the civil war histories and pulp westerns he loved before the stroke. Mom says he doesn't want to read anymore. She tries to get him interested in books, but he never makes it past the first few pages. My father says reading takes too much concentration. She pushes, he refuses. She lets it go.

*

My mother's words about my father's refusal to read make me anxious, panicky. Not long after the stroke, I helped my father with one of his occupational therapy assignments: looking up a series of business names in the yellow pages and noting their phone numbers on a worksheet, an activity designed to strengthen cognitive sorting and sequencing capabilities diminished by stroke. I waited at the kitchen table while my father struggled to look up the entries and record the numbers in the correct order, sometimes confusing the phone numbers, other times confusing the sequence of the alphabet.

My mind flashed to this same scene, 30 years earlier. My father and I sat at the kitchen table. I struggled to remember my times tables. My father waited impatiently. He could do complex math in his sleep, while I couldn't seem to fix even the simplest operations in my memory. I looked at the problems on the page and the numbers danced before my eyes. My father insisted that I stay at the table until I finished every last problem. "Finish it now. Don't leave it until later," he'd say.

That day at the kitchen table, I urged my father to keep looking up names and numbers in the phone book.

"Only three more!" I said, forcing a smile.

My father closed the phone book and pushed it away with his working right hand. "I'm tired honey. Let's finish it later."

"Don't you want to finish it now?" I pushed.

He reached for his cane. "No. I don't need the phone number of a lawn mower repair guy. Hell, I can't even use the lawn mower."

I didn't say anything. I let him go.

I think now about how loss hits us in waves.[20] From our earliest moments we are taught to begin each endeavor, including grieving, with an aim, a project, a plan. What we don't teach ourselves, or others, is how easily these aims, projects, and plans can change, evaporate, and create a suddenly present absence. How easily we are frustrated, felled. How we are suddenly exhausted but do not know why.

*

I don't want to let reading go. I don't want to let my father go. After dinner, my father uses his cane to make the short trip from the dining room to his recliner and begins watching a baseball game on television. My mother and I do the dishes. "I have an idea," I say.

"What's that?" Mom asks.

My daughter has a list of books to read over the summer and I've resolved to help her work on building her reading comprehension. I seize on an opportunity to include my father, to help him return to reading and strengthen his relationship with my daughter. "What if I send Dad the next book on our summer reading list? Dad could read it and they could talk about the story. It would encourage them both to read and would give them something to talk about. They could talk every few days."

"That would be great," Mom says. "But I don't know if Dad will stick with it. He gets so frustrated."

"I don't think the book will be too challenging—it's on the incoming 5th grade summer reading list. If Dad thought he were helping with her homework, I bet he'd do it."

"It's worth a try. Send the book."

*

A week later, my father calls me. "I'm not sure what you want me to do with this book," he says.

"I need your help. I was hoping you'd read a book on her summer reading list and then talk to her about the story. You'd be helping with her homework.

"You never liked me helping *you* with *your* homework."

"I passed all my math classes, didn't I?"

"Well sure. I could do math."

"You could read too! So, will you help her out?"

"I'll try honey."

*

My daughter reads the first few chapters of *A Wrinkle in Time*, a story about a brilliant scientist father who goes missing and the strange and stubborn daughter who sets out to find him. She calls my father. She listens while he talks. She says "Ya," "Okay," Sure." She holds the phone out to me. "Grandpa wants to talk to you."

"Hi Dad, how are you?"

"Not too good."

"No? What's not too good?"

"I can't help with this book, honey."

"You can't?"

"No. I've read the first chapter several times, but I can't remember what happens."

"Oh, Dad, that's okay."

"My brain just doesn't work as well as it used to."

"I've read that first chapter and it's confusing."

"It's not confusing for you, but it is for me. I used to be able to read anything, but now I can't. Tell her I won't be able to help with her homework."

"Don't worry, Dad. I can help her. I've never read *A Wrinkle in Time*, and I should.

"I'm sorry."

"No, *I'm sorry*. I didn't mean for this to be a frustrating experience for you."

"I just don't read much anymore. But honey?"

"Yes?"

"Make sure she finishes that book."

"I'll make sure she finishes it. We both will."

*

My daughter enjoys *A Wrinkle in Time*, particularly the character Charles Wallace, who sees, knows, and understands what Meg, the daughter in search of her father, cannot.

I enjoy the story too, particularly the story of Mr. Murry, Meg's father. What intrigues me most about this story is not his character—Mr. Murry, the person— but instead the idea of his being lost. Where he went and why remain a mystery for most of the story; something is hiding in the loss of him, something is lost within the recesses of this loss.[21] When he is found, Mr. Murry is nearly unrecognizable, and yet Meg doesn't question that he is her father, despite his having changed, despite his inability to right everything wrong in the world.[22] Instead, Meg forgives him[23]—and herself—for wanting to both disavow and control who she and her father are and what they mean together.[24] I close the book lying open in my hands. There is losing; and there is the transformative effect of loss. Neither can be planned or charted.[25]

NOTES

[1] L'Engle (1962, p. 171).

[2] Butler (2004, p. 26): "There is bound to be some experience of humiliation for adults, who think that they are exercising judgment in matters of love, to reflect upon the fact that, as infants and young children, they loved their parents or other primary others in absolute and uncritical ways—and that something of that pattern lives on in their adult relationships."

[3] Butler (2004, p. 46): "I find that my very formation implicates the other in me, that my own foreignness to myself is, paradoxically, the source of my ethical connection with others. I am not fully known to myself, because part of what I am is the enigmatic traces of others."

[4] Adams (2012, p. 194). My father's words to me are both protective—it's your decision, I want you to be happy, that's all that matters—and dismissive—I don't understand it, I don't think it's right. Like Adams, I "long for a more engaging response. I want him to comment on my sexuality, to recognize and respect it. But I say nothing."

[5] Butler (2005, pp. 112-113): "Foucault reads confession as an act of speech in which the subject 'publishes [her]self,' gives [her]self in words ... as a way of making the self appear for another."

[6] Butler (2004, p. 20): "Loss and vulnerability seem to follow from our being socially constituted bodies, attached to others, at risk of losing those attachments ...."

[7] L'Engle (1962, p. 160).

[8] Stroke Association (2012, pp. 1-2): The physical changes created as a result of stroke include weakness and paralysis, loss of balance, muscle stiffness and pain, changes in physical sensitivity, and difficulties speaking and swallowing. In addition to these physical effects, strokes also have cognitive, emotional, and relational impacts. Mukherjee, Levin, and Heller (2006, p. 26) note that these effects include depression and anxiety, changes in identity and personality, changes in social roles and family dynamics, social isolation, and communication difficulties.

[9] Mukherjee, Levin, and Heller (2006, p. 28): Stroke often affects the executive functions of the brain, including "cognitive control, cognitive set-shifting, and sequencing a series of events."

[10] Butler (2004, p. 20).

[11] Mukherjee, Levin, and Heller (2006, p. 28): Comments about changes in identity post-stroke are telling, in terms of not only my father's experience of self post-stroke, but also my own experience of self post-coming out and of my relationship with my father post-stroke *and* post coming-out: "A common experience after brain injury is a radical break in the flow of identity, often due to the loss of skills or activities that were profoundly intertwined with the individual's sense of self .... Accepting the loss of identities that were previously crucial to one's sense of self and inventing new ones that provide satisfaction and fulfillment are key to adjustment."

[12] Butler (2004, p. 27): "I may wish to reconstitute my 'self' as if it were there all along, a tacit ego with acumen from the start; but to do so would be to deny the various forms of rapture and subjection that formed the condition of my emergence as an individual being and that continue to haunt my adult sense of self with whatever anxiety and longing I may now feel."

[13] Butler (2004, p. 32).

[14] L'Engle (1962, pp. 165-166).

[15] Butler (2004, p. 44): "When we recognize another, or when we ask for recognition for ourselves, we are not asking for an Other to see us as we are, as we already are, as we always have been, as we were constituted prior to the encounter itself."

[16] Butler (2004, p. 44): "Instead, in the asking, in the petition, we have already become something new, since we are constituted by virtue of the address …. To ask for recognition, or to offer it, is precisely not to ask for recognition for what one already is. It is to solicit a becoming, to instigate a transformation, to petition the future always in relation to the other."

[17] Wyatt (2012, p. 165): "Familiar stories become strange. Loss written and rewritten."

[18] Butler (2004, p. 44).

[19] L'Engle (1962, p. 221).

[20] Butler (2004, p. 21): "I think one is hit by waves, that one starts out the day with an aim, a project, a plan, and finds oneself foiled. One finds oneself fallen. One is exhausted but one does know why."

[21] Butler (2004, pp. 21-22): "Freud reminded us that when we lose someone, we do not always know what it is *in* that person that has been lost. So when one loses, one is also faced with something enigmatic: something is hiding in the loss, something is lost within the recesses of loss."

[22] L'Engle (1962, pp. 174-176): "She had been so certain that at the moment she found her father everything would be all right. Everything would be settled …. Her father had been found but had not made everything all right. Instead everything was worse than ever, and her adored father was bearded and thin and white and not omnipotent at all."

[23] L'Engle (1962, p. 220): "At last she turned to her father. 'I'm—I'm sorry Father … I wanted you to do it all for me. I wanted everything to be all easy and simple."

[24] Butler (2004, p. 28): "Let us return to the issue of grief, to the moments in which one undergoes something outside one's control and finds that one is beside oneself, not at one with oneself. Perhaps we can say that grief contains the possibility of apprehending a mode of dispossession that is fundamental to who I am … we are, from the start and by virtue of being a bodily being, already given over, beyond ourselves, implicated in lives that our not our own."

[25] Butler (2004, p. 21).

REFERENCES

Adams, T. E. (2012). Missing each other. *Qualitative Inquiry, 18*, 193-196.

Butler, J. (2004). *Precarious life: The powers of mourning and violence.* London: Verso.

Butler, J. (2005). *Giving an account of oneself.* New York: Fordham University Press.

L'Engle, M. (1962). *A wrinkle in time.* New York: Farrar, Straus, Giroux.

Mukherjee, D., Levin, R.L, & Heller, W. (2006). The cognitive, emotional, and social sequelae of stroke: Psychological and ethical concerns in post-stroke adaptation. *Topics in Stroke Rehabilitation, 13*, 26-35.

Stroke Association. *The physical effects of stroke.* Accessed June 15, 2013 from http://www.stroke.org.uk/sites/default/files/Physical%20effects%20of%20stroke.pdf

Wyatt, J. (2012). Fathers, sons, loss, and the search for the question. *Qualitative Inquiry, 18*, 162-167.

Stacy Holman Jones
Department of Communication Studies
California State University, Northridge

CRAIG GINGRICH-PHILBROOK

ON GRATITUDE, FOR MY FATHER

I

The father's day remembrances go up across Facebook, released like doves at a funeral or little fires set in paper boats and pushed out into the way time flows and eddies. Something rises in an up-draft, something circles and burns on the surface in the dark. I think about oxygen and time, "fuel for the fire," ritual—all the things consumed and all the transformed materials left in their wake: ash, rust, a sudden turbulence in the air, a diminishing memory of the sound made by something or someone coming loose from an anchor in the present. I write his name on the screen in electricity and sand: *Paul Llewelyn Philbrook*. Something disappears, something persists, something changes—the universe as resolute and capricious in its self-differing as ever. In the midst of such remembrances, I realize I will think of this as the summer I made my peace with mint.

For thirty-nine years, I have had an indecorous relationship with mint. I tell you about it because it helps me explain the preservation of injury in sense memory and the body. My problem with mint started in the front yard of the house in Burney, California, where I lived for part of the year I turned twelve. It's April 1974. My father and grandfather have come out into the yard, heading over to the woodpile at the other side of the house. They begin taking logs apart with a chainsaw, a sledgehammer, and a wedge.

One could take an inventory of the senses, here: the warmth of the sun falls against my face, for example, striated by the long shadows of pine trees, the tall kind, a forest of them across the street where the wilderness begins. The sound of the chainsaw obscures the periodic anvil ring of the sledgehammer on the dark metal wedge—a small note sitting back in the mix behind the engine's blurry roar. The smell of exhaust competes with the tang of the wet, splitting wood.

But all of that temperature and sound and smell comes from over there. When I locate what I used to think of as my own body, over here in the memory, I find it bent into the long planter running along the front of the house. Although some distance away from my father and grandfather, I inhabit their lines of sight. I find myself wanting to say that it was not yet my body bent over into that planter, that the incarnate speaking function I think of as "I" had not yet acquired a signature loss that haunts its cognitive registers. That other body, that other boy, smells the damp mud and plucks a few leaves of the mint growing wild there, rolls them to bite between his teeth and tongue as his mother has taught him to do, rinsing them first beneath the faucet that comes out of the siding of the house and drips. Something cold happens, something simultaneously clean feeling and yet musky,

J. Wyatt & T. E. Adams (eds.), On (Writing) Families, 23–29.

earthy, when he bites through them, delicately, over and over again, scoring the roll of leaves on his tongue to free the oils and compounds to do what they do against the most dexterous part of his body, after his hands.

I've tipped you off, of course, that something bad happens, but let's not hurry out of this suspended time. At this moment, he doesn't know what happens next, and the loss of that innocence will change him into me. It's a literary conceit, to put it this way, but it would also require a conceit to pretend I know what he thought about as he rose and stood there, watching our father and grandfather across the yard. If I had to, I'd bet it was probably something about animals or crafts or how unsafe he felt at school—he's not a complete innocent, by any means. One loses innocence, like the closet, in stages. With our grandparents visiting, though, he probably felt at least a little happy.

And then the sound of the chainsaw digs into the ground, our father falls, and our grandfather bends over the body in the sawdust; the boy's teeth go through the mint and into my tongue because, seeing Dad fall like that, he lost track of what the panicked flesh becoming my body was doing.

There are some other things I don't know yet—that my father has had a brain hemorrhage, for example, or that he will die in a few days. I have different fears. I think Dad has cut into himself. I run into the house shouting for my mother or grandmother to call an ambulance. I go to my room and fall on my knees to pray at the edge of the bed. In a way, I resemble a *Precious Moments* figurine, I suppose, or a Norman Rockwell painting, if someone pushed them over a few panicked clicks toward the surreal side. My eyes clamp closed. My tongue tries to put sentences together. Dramatic irony complicates my memory now, because I know the praying doesn't "work," but at the time I want to do the right thing because I think it might. I want to remember, for example, the requisite phrase of humility my mother has taught me to say: "Thy will be done," always right before "in Jesus's name, Amen." But I don't recall stopping; the memory ends there, with me praying, begging, really—almost singing, almost ringing out beneath this blow driving me deeper into something: perhaps that innocence we spoke of earlier, splitting finally apart.

For years, I hated mint, but mint is hard to avoid. Spearmint was the worst. I went through an Altoid peppermint phase when I lived in New York, for what that's worth—maybe just to have something to do on the subway rather than attending to anyone around me, feeling like a bumpkin in a strange machine. For the most part, though, I rejected mint at every turn, searching out toothpaste flavored with more appealing imitations (watermelon kid's toothpaste, orange, cinnamon); I did not want to go back to that front yard every day of my life. This habit of rejection became an odd shield against teleportation there, against the inevitable short circuit of before and after that made me feel only tenuously connected to the present, never quite reconstituting or remaining on either side of mint's transporter beam.

2

I want to say that, unlike men who had their father well into their adult lives, I have primarily an imaginary relationship with mine, peppered by bits and pieces brought back unexpectedly, forcefully, by strange things—the taste of mint, for example. But I believe I know, although I cannot know, that most people experience their fathers precisely this way: as imaginary beings. Losing my dad when I was twelve years old did many of the things you might expect it did, each of them complicated: complicated by my mother's alterations of her stories about who he was, changing her depiction of him to suit her need to control my self-perception at any given moment; complicated by broad cultural narratives about the consequences of fatherlessness on boys and their sexuality; complicated by my fortunes with the father-surrogates among my coaches and teachers. I did my best to protect these men from the vacuum-force of my father hunger, but I often failed.

Certain competitive logics of loss and genres of storytelling ask me to compare wounds, to say that, unlike those men lucky enough to have fathers as they grew up, I had a difficult time: I invented, I struggled to belong, I had no one to do this or that with me. But, while I did have a hard time, fall back on invention, and struggle to belong, I will not assert the preeminence of my difficulty over that of these men with their living fathers; I can't presume to know about them. What I have learned most in this life is that, if there is something stranger than a ghost, it is a living person. I must, then, also acknowledge that losing my dad at twelve years old freed me from his surveillance and the terror of receiving or losing his approval on a daily basis. His death made some aspects of that terror moot and cast me loose among my own devices. It remains entirely possible that losing my father was the best thing that ever happened, the constitutive prerequisite for the person I think of loosely as "me."

So I have no idea, really, about fathers, least of all my own, in any terms, comparative or otherwise, that I trust; I have inclinations toward positions, but I find these epistemologically insufficient as soon as I recognize myself sliding into them. My father and his absence have almost always been present, and they have always been changing. I can offer this essay only as a demonstration of the perpetuation of his uncertain function, its condensations and displacements, and the way I sometimes feel the long presence of his absence drag me around the way wind drags an old leaf. The wind shows little concern for the dangers of the human world, like oncoming traffic, when it pulls a leaf precariously across a busy street. Likewise, my father's absence shows no regard for when and where it tugs on my sleeve and says, "Come along." In these pages I can only tug, in a reversal of roles, at him, at his absence, and say, "No, no; *you* come with me. We have work to do."

Our work boils down to making sense of this: almost every adult relative has told me, at some point, *"Your father would be so proud of you."* Each of my debate coaches did, and a beloved English teacher. I am supposed to want this knowledge, to require this reassurance that his feelings for me were neither neutral nor shame. These reassurers forget that he died before his body became off limits to me. I remember the feel of his beard, the good-night kisses, waking over his shoulder as he carried me to bed the many nights I fell asleep in the living room. I miss his body because his sudden disappearance took it from me, whole, not because I endured its withering away under the glaring surveillance of heteronormative propriety. I have not had to sit across the table from him as an adult and long for that lost contact with his body. For this, I have gratitude.

Nonetheless, I acknowledge my uncertainty about his pride. I acknowledge that, in this ambiguity, when my coaches and teachers said it, when my coaches and teachers who actually took the time to know me said he would be proud, sometimes even that they themselves would be proud to have me as a son, I felt faint. I felt I might swoon.

I had reason to feel uncertain.

3

My mother made a slumber party for my tenth birthday. She wanted to normalize my relationships among the boys in my class. These boys had spent the last year calling me "sissy" as if it were my name. I'd endured a horrible compulsory little league season with them, meant to compensate for or force me to acquire the masculinity my fourth-grade teacher called a conference with my parents to convince them that I lacked. The grade before, my friend Joe essentially said goodbye to me, telling me that he didn't know how to be my friend anymore because I didn't act like a boy, and I didn't act like a girl. Even though he liked me, he just didn't know what to do with me. *He just didn't know what to do.* We were off script, in other words, and he didn't care to improvise.

I have two memories from this birthday slumber party, I just don't remember which came first, the chicken or the cake. The boys and I were outside playing at twilight. They tied me to a board on the ground by the barn and left me there. Alone in the rising darkness, I looked to my side and saw my chicken, Red, dead in the long grass by my face. I don't think they killed her; I think they didn't see her there in the twilight. I do not know how long I laid there with her, struggling against the ropes and the rough wood. The memory ends, seeing her.

And then later, or before, who can say, we sat around the dining-room table, all clustered together, having ice cream and cake. Me and these boys who called me sissy. Me and these boys who had just tied, or would soon tie, me to a board and leave me by my dead friend. My dad came up behind me and pushed me down into my plate, pushed my face down into my plate. I'm sure he was just being jocular, and everyone was supposed to know that. I'm sure I did my best to be, as they say, a good sport. But I can't really tell you what happened next. The impression that remains is that he was now one of them, that he joined them in their orientation toward me as a degradable object.

[At this moment early in drafting this essay, Sparklehorse's jangly folktronica cover of "Galveston" comes on my headphones. I begin dancing in my chair, distant, dissociative, disappearing in a joyous fog. The high-tech mesh beneath me bounces like the seat of my dad's truck down the gravel roads around Standish, California, population 54. We moved a lot. The Glen Campbell original, which he loved, is on the radio in the other layer, in the other time stream, in my imagination. Dad is happy, and I am not unhappy. For this, I have gratitude.]

At some point, in my twenties or thirties or forties, who can say—perhaps even several times over those years—I told my mother the story about the cake. I would like to say she did not remember; the conventions of this sort of narrative suggest that, if she did not remember, the story's antagonist-protagonist relationship might snap into focus. But I don't know. It would have been like her, in her own fog under the weight of the Codeine and Valium and Robaxin she had by then become addicted to, not to remember that he had done this to me. It would have been like her, she who mostly felt injured by, and resisted, this sort of detail, the way a body festers around a splinter to push the offense out of its flesh.

But this convention casts her as my aggressor, as refusing what my body and I knew to be true. I want to acknowledge that, at least sometimes in telling her this story, I must have hurled it aggressively *at her*, as injury, as a way to counter or at least to test her claims about my father and his pride, to burn those claims to the ground, to see what remained. It would have been like me, me who, also, *mostly felt injured by and resisted this sort of detail the way a child's body festers around a splinter to push the offense out of its flesh.*

After at least one of these incidents when my mother and I exchanged our information and lack thereof about the cake and the face involved, she told me that she had, around that time, in conversation with Dad about the sissy problem, told him about her gay cousin, Michael, who lived in San Francisco. Let's call it 1972. Apparently Dad then "made a joke" that, if he'd known about Michael, he would never have married her. She chose to tell me that. I'm sure he was just being jocular, and she and I were supposed to know that. I'm sure we did our bests to be, as they say, good sports. Mom believed the joke helped explain his motivation for sending me back to school on the swollen, bruised feet the bullies left behind one day in seventh grade. It was two years after the party, two towns and two schools removed. They gathered, held me against a hallway wall and took turns stomping on my feet, demanding that I admit I was queer, a word I did not entirely understand, then—or now, frankly, depending upon the finality we do or do not require for uses of the word "understand." I was in seventh grade, at the combined middle and high school in Burney. Burney is a somewhat larger town than Standish, to be sure, but hardly a tolerant, cosmopolitan metropolis. It took a long time to get the boots off when I hobbled home for lunch, having never considered going to the nurse or any other adult for help, so used to this kind of thing by then and not having been asked, by anyone, why I couldn't seem to walk. Mom wanted to cut the boots off, but they belonged to my father, and he loved them, so I wouldn't let her (Gingrich-Philbrook, 1997).

4

The only reason I can think of for my parents not taking me to the doctor is their shame. We went to the doctor for lesser things. I grew up with and on these aching feet, and I still fight that shame in my shoes. This part of me *is* this injury, and, just as a flash of mint can take me back to the yard, when my feet get bad and each step sends a bolt of pain up my leg, I think back to that soon-to-be-fatherless boy held against the wall in that hallway. I said that to my friend and colleague Ron Pelias, reflecting on what some might consider my overreaction to the bullying of queer performance artist Tim Miller by the Catholic Newman Society and the President of the Catholic University Villanova, who banned him from campus. Villanova's speech department, Tim's hosts, made no statement in Tim's defense and at least appeared to tell individual faculty to keep from doing so on their own (Gingrich-Philbrook, 2013; Gingrich-Philbrook & Gray, 2013). I told Ron I didn't think people understood what it was like to feel in every step a painful reminder of being bullied for who they were, or how it felt to worry, every day, with empathy and sense memory, about queer kids. I still don't think they know what it's like to detest the church that licenses the hate driving these children's attackers with words like "abomination." Tim Miller fights back for these kids, fights back against that hate every day. Restimulations of such injury appear in ways we can't easily identify as simply either wrong (the habit of inappropriate projection of the past into the present) or right (the productive transmission of past wisdom into a current circumstance).

I put my head on Ron's shoulder.

"Why didn't you defend yourself?" my folks asked, over and over again at the dinner table that night, passing the potatoes and the gravy and the buck for that shame. The fact that there were five or more boys and that they were five years older and taller and stronger didn't faze them.

I got the impression they would have taken me to the doctor if I'd fought back. What does it mean for a kid to get such an impression?

Some consider my call that performance studies scholars protest the "Ethics and Economies of Performance" conference at Villanova out of scale. Even after the President's ugly acquiescence to the Newman Society's lies about Tim, they think that my protest is too much. I consider it an act of defending queer performance and all of those who do it and all of those we do it for from coast to coast. Because when I take those painful steps, I don't think just about the bullies. They were kids with their own fears and fathers. I think about the grown ups—teachers, my parents, everybody—who *did nothing*. I have grown tired of all the nothing. All the "evolution." All the too little, all the too late. All the leaving us to defend ourselves and freaking the fuck out when we finally do.

5

My partner in life and a civil union, Jonny Gray, has taught me many things. He loves mint. One could make too much of this, so let me just put it simply. With time, I have watched him enjoy mint, and it's gotten easier to do so, myself, to make room for other things mint might offer. I've started cooking with it more often. He planted a bunch of it, several different varieties, in a garden this summer. I even sort of invented a good way to enjoy mint: mince it, steep it in a glass of fruit juice in the refrigerator for a day, and then add a small bit of it to some seltzer or iced tea.

I don't mean this to suggest that I've undertaken a desensitization program, although it has a similar structure, I suppose. I haven't forgotten that day in the yard, by any means. But I'm less subject to its whims, to its violent return. Now, it feels more like I get to say, "Oh, yeah, there you are again. How have you been, morning on the lawn? What have you been up to, these days, 1974?"

6

Alongside these and other absences, I summon the memory of a particular night, just weeks before my father died. Like so many other nights, I wake with my head on his shoulder as he carries me to bed. It happens just a few weeks after or before my parents do not take me to the doctor about my feet. I can't say which came first, whether that bashing is or is not on my Father's mind as he bears me to bed. There's a photo in our family album from that night. I'm sleeping in a green recliner, arms and legs akimbo in pajamas with little horses on them. I can imagine my parents deciding to get the camera, to take the photo, one of those last, "isn't it cute where our little boy fell asleep" pictures people snap to memorialize a child's body before it disappears forever in the push out of itself into something that, or someone who, terrifies them with its difference.

There is no picture of my feet.

I wake. I wake on his shoulder.

The warmth of his body radiates from his flesh to mine, the scruff of his beard rough against me as I cling to his shoulder. Part of me still lives there, my face, my face turned in, my face pressing down into the crook of his neck among the smell of nicotine and salt and sandalwood cologne. He moves gently under the weight of his queer burden, careful with me, whispering goodnight to the boy he helped to make, kissing me.

For this memory, I have gratitude.

I choose not to defend myself against it.

I let it be what it will be, parting my lips for the cold glass in my hand.

REFERENCES

Gingrich-Philbrook, C. (1997) Refreshment. *Text and Performance Quarterly, 17,* 352-360.

Gingrich-Philbrook, C. (2013). Evaluating (evaluations of) autoethnography. In S. Holman Jones, T. E. Adams, & C. Ellis (Eds.), *Handbook of autoethnography* (pp. 609-626). Walnut Creek, CA: Left Coast Press.

Gingrich-Philbrook, C., & Gray, J. (2013). A counterweight to silence: What resistance remains. *Text and Performance Quarterly, 33,* 238-243.

Craig Gingrich-Philbrook
Department of Speech Communication
Southern Illinois University Carbondale

PATRICIA LEAVY

CONFESSIONS OF A FEMINIST MOTHER RAISING A PRETEEN DAUGHTER

As I write this my 12-year-old daughter, Madeline, is in her bedroom. I don't think she sees me as the enemy at this particular moment, although sometimes she does. I seem to vacillate between friend, confidant, frenemy and enemy—and I'm often not sure why my status shifts. As for what she's doing in her room, I'm really not sure, but most likely it's one of the following: hanging out on social media with her friends (a true mix of "good girls" and "mean girls"), following an online makeup or hairstyling tutorial, listening to music (which could range from One Direction to Rihanna to Britney Spears), reading, writing or making art. As you might imagine, I prefer some of these activities more than others.

This essay is about my evolving struggle to reconcile my feminist standpoint, my own personal preferences and my parenting of a preteen girl. Let me start by telling you a little about who I am.

I was born feminist. I know that feminism is an earned achievement, and that there is value added for life experience, exposure to inequalities, immersion in feminist scholarship, participation in activist activities, and building bonds with other feminists. Nevertheless, I also know that I was born feminist, or more accurately, I can't recall a time when I wasn't feminist. For me, feminism has an anti-racist, anti-homophobic and anti-classist agenda as much as it has an anti-sexist one. Growing up there were signs of my feminism.

From the time I was three years old my parents belonged to a private country club. I learned at a very young age that my father was the true member, and through him my mother, sisters and I. Women were not allowed to be members. I was deeply troubled by this discovery made at the age of five or six when I questioned the nuances of the language my parents used to talk about membership. They spouted all kinds of justifications of "this wasn't a big deal," but to me it was. I soon became the outcast in my family by pointing this out and "complaining" about it regularly. Although it no longer is, the country club was also all white when I was growing up. When I made this discovery around the age of 10, I loudly asked my parents, in the crowded dining room of the club: "Where are all of the African-American people?" There was quite a gasp. I believe they were embarrassed, and so was I, although for different reasons. Again, the justifications came, although this time they were whispered. "No one has been kept out, it's just that only white people have applied to get in." Only a few years later I would refuse to go to the club on the basis that it was racist, and I missed a great deal of "family time" as a result. In fairness to my parents, I should note that eventually an African-American family applied for membership to the exclusive club. My parents developed a friendship with them and sponsored their bid to get into the club. My father threatened to quit the club if they weren't admitted, which would clearly have been on the basis of race. They were admitted. Women are members now too; even single women. Although more politically correct, I still consider it an elitist, sexist and racist environment and don't expect I'll ever be there again. I have many other examples of my feminism during my teen years. For example, I participated in a walkout in high school to attend a pro-choice rally in Boston. Much to the chagrin of my parents (who incidentally are pro-choice), I returned to decorate my room with clothing hangers bearing the message "this is not a surgical instrument, keep abortion safe and legal."

In my adult life my commitment to feminism has only deepened, and I devoted more than 12 years to teaching feminist sociology courses, founding a gender and sexualities studies program at a conservative Catholic college where I also served as PRIDE advisor, conducting scholarly research on gender, race and sexual identity, writing feminist fiction and public writing and speaking on issues pertaining to the lives of girls and women. Like other feminists, I've contended with my share of hate and ignorance from vandalized materials on my office bulletin board to the nasty-grams my op-eds routinely inspire.

All of this is by way of telling you that I feel committed to feminism. However, this is only part of who I am. I am also a woman who wears makeup (even to go to the grocery store), has a closet full of high heels and trendy clothes, drives two hours to get my hair done at the salon that does it "right" and consumes some of the same commercial media I would critique in a sociology of gender course.

There's often a disjuncture between theoretical/social ideals and the reality of our lives—where each of us draws the line between a sexist joke we're laughing along with, and one we are protesting. It is through the experience of raising Madeline that I feel most confronted with the gap between my feminist ideals and my personal preferences (which as a sociologist I know are shaped by the culture in which I live).

From the time Madeline was born I was aware of my responsibility to socialize her, knowing she would internalize many of the messages I sent through both my words and actions. Feminist ideals would be a core part of the value system with which she was raised. To me this has always meant two things: teaching her about social justice and giving her the tools for empowerment. The latter has proved far more challenging.

Giving her a social justice perspective has always been a conscious choice. For example, I have never shied away from discussions of sexism, racism, homophobia or classism. More than that, I have taken it as my responsibility to celebrate diversity in her life—from the books and dolls waiting in her room when she came home from the hospital, to the people welcomed into her life and the language used to talk about love and hate. And I know I have done at least some things well. She has shown over and over again that she finds "-isms" intolerable. This started when she was quite young.

When she was about seven years old we took a trip to Story Land in New Hampshire. While we were in the car the following conversation ensued:

Madeline: Someone was teased in school the other day.
Me: How?
Madeline: Some kids called him gay.
I turned around and opened my mouth but before I could say anything ...
Madeline: I know it's not a bad word, but they think it is.

There are more recent examples of her reporting kids in her middle school who have used homophobic or racial slurs, even when her doing so came at a personal cost. Despite her strong ethical compass and willingness to stand up for others, when it comes to empowerment and issues of gender, femininity, body image and sexism, I am plagued by tensions and even failures as much as what I perceive as "successes." Sometimes I think all of this was easier when Madeline was younger.

From the time Madeline was very little I taught her that Barbie was bad. Yes, I'm one of those crazy feminist sociologist mothers who told her daughter that Barbie is in fact bad. As a result, I endured toward quite a bit of ridicule within my own family. My parents and siblings diminished my parenting choice and even purchased Barbies for my daughter despite my explicit instructions. But I had taught Madeline well. When she was just a few years old, and still in her stroller, my laptop computer died and I went to a store to buy a new one. On a tight budget and with no tech knowledge whatsoever, this was a long process. Madeline sat patiently in her stroller while a sales clerk assisted me. He was so impressed with Madeline's behavior during the long ordeal that when he went to get my laptop from the back he also brought a present for her: he handed her a Barbie computer game. She looked at it, looked up at him, and most innocently replied: "Thank you, man, but Barbie is bad for the children and I'm a children." She held the game out to return it and he looked at me quite confused. But times change. A year or two later she would ask me for a Barbie sticker book while browsing around a Borders bookstore. I replied: "I don't like Barbie because I think that she sends bad messages to girls about what girls are supposed to look like, but I promised I would buy you something and if this is what you want, you can have it." She looked at the sticker book again and then put it down, deciding on a Scooby Doo sticker book instead. Not long after that she would select a Barbie product or two, which I bought for her, only to discover that she really didn't have any interest in Barbie— she found Barbie boring.

Despite these early "successes" in marrying my feminist principles to my parenting strategies, the marrying was only going to become more difficult. The fact that when I was little I had a drawer filled with Barbies and as an adult a closet full of what could easily be Barbie's clothing, which would make my embodiment of femininity bump against feminist mothering. Perhaps nothing highlights this more for me than the experience of seeing *Part of Me*, the Katy Perry movie, with Madeline.

Madeline is a fan of Katy Perry's music (at least she was at the time we saw the film; attitudes change so quickly at this age). She asked me to take her to see the movie. Frankly I thought it would be more fun than some of the other things she likes to see, and I was happy to spend the time alone with her. We loved the movie and found ourselves humming along and swaying to the tunes, which were mostly new to me. What I most enjoyed was the backstage access to Perry's life as a commercial artist, from her early days to her record-breaking world tour. I'm always interested in the behind-the-scenes of women in the arts. What Madeline enjoyed most was getting to see Katy Perry's costumes and candy-land set design—as most of the movie followed her tour. After the movie Madeline asked me if I liked it and I was quick to say that I did. She then told me that she loved Perry's costumes and asked if I did as well. What was I to say? The truth was, I found the costumes very aesthetically pleasing: they were fun, pretty and fantasy filled. However, they were also hyper-sexualized and infantilizing—not a good message for young girls. In the moment before I answered, I was also negotiating the complex reality of trying to relate with my daughter and find pleasure in what she finds pleasure in while also giving her the tools to critique sexist ideologies. I told her that I thought the costumes were cool because she was on stage performing, but I didn't think they were appropriate for real girls or women in everyday life.

We went home blaring Perry's CD, both of us singing along to quasi-feminist anthems, just trying to enjoy the moment.

I'm sure I'm not the only mother who experienced this conundrum and I acknowledge I can only write about it from my point of view. A quick glance on social media shows that Katy Perry is a polarizing force for many feminists. She is a quintessential success story of a woman in pop culture with an entire empire built around the self-proclaimed "Candy Queen." Perry has broken long-standing billboard records held by men, toured the world on her own successes, and written many songs about female empowerment. Perry also costumes herself in everything from lingerie to hyper-sexualized sugary confections, even going so far as to pose in a silver cupcake wrapper dress, a peppermint striped costume with strategically placed twirling candies, and the classic black leather "cat costume." Predictably, Perry has publicly denounced feminism. None of this is surprising in the world of commercial pop culture, although it is in many ways sad. But it doesn't stop me from enjoying her music and continuing to listen to it in the car and at home, along with Madeline. I hope the images and messages are mediated by the feminist music that is also a staple in our life.

For example, Madeline has been going to Tori Amos concerts since she was seven years old. She has met Tori Amos and Paula Cole and their music fills our house far more frequently than anything in the top 40 genre. I also have ongoing conversations with Madeline about artistry—writing, producing and playing one's own music—versus the world of commercial pop. The self-presentation of female artists is always a part of this conversation. And while I believe Madeline would put on Perry's twirling peppermint candy dress in a heartbeat, I am also convinced that she is able to distinguish between different kinds of female artists and make very wise determinations about role models.

I know the tensions I experience living and reflecting my feminist principles are still largely down the road for Madeline. There will be struggles with body acceptance, self-expression and sexuality that will test her esteem and, perhaps, create tensions in her identity that she will have to learn to negotiate. As she carves her own identity, our relationship will continue to shift and evolve, and I have no doubt the hardest years for us are also ahead. Perhaps all mothers mostly wish to be lifelong friends with their daughters, which is how I envision us. If I'm brutally honest, I hope to have raised someone I will want to be friends with, who will want the same with me. But I know that I will need to support and accept Madeline if she is going to choose to maintain a close relationship. As she continues to grow into herself, discover her gifts and confront her challenges, I will be there to support her. I am confident that she is a good person. I respect her. I believe there is a mutual respect we have cultivated that will help our future together. In the end, I believe that respect is the greatest gift my feminist parenting has generated.

Just a few days ago during a car ride, Madeline described a music video by Pink for a song called *Stupid Girls*. She told me in great detail about the video images and lyrics, which in essence expose and challenge dominant representations of femininity, from a well-known Jessica Simpson video, in which the scantily clad star douses herself with water under the pretense of washing a car, to the culture's obsession with plastic surgery. A young girl featured in this music video is portrayed learning Pink's lessons. In the end she tunes out of commercial culture and picks up a football to go outside and play. Madeline told me she knew I would like the video and song because I teach and write about these issues. Later, when we got home, she desperately wanted to show me the video and so we watched it together. She was on target about the messages and although it's not my preferred style of music, I thought it was terrific for all of the reasons she had noted. I have to confess, I wasn't only delighted that she recognized the messages of dominant culture and how this was a powerful and direct counter message. It was also clear that she was trying to impress me with her awareness of these issues, which to me means that even if she's searching through the linen closet for my old makeup and asking me to straighten her hair, she knows what's important to me—and that's important to her.

Patricia Leavy
Independent Scholar
www.patricialeavy.com

DESIRÉE D. ROWE

ROSES AND GRIME

Tattoos, Texts, and Failure

"Ever tried. Ever failed. No matter. Try again. Fail again. Fail better."
—Samuel Beckett, *Worstward Ho*

There is a print in my office of this quote. I stop, occasionally, to think of what it means to others. In relation.

The framed print hangs next to an 8x11 color photograph. The spatial proximity between the photo and print are important to me. The photo is an enlarged image of my father Al's bicep. I bought a gaudy shiny black frame to offset the rugged masculinity of the image—a big muscular, hairy arm. At the very top of the picture you can see two of my father's fingers as he lifts up the sleeve of his shirt.

Those hands. The story of my relationship with my father is long. Too long for me and you now, but sometimes I think it is a narrative all too familiar. I can say keywords and you can put it together, right? Drinking, yelling, divorce, single mom. Damn. Sometimes I feel like I live a clichéd life.

My father has worked as a mechanic since he was 14. His hands show the years. Cracked with perpetually black fingernails. Always. I can imagine that the same dirt that was there on the day of my birth will be there until the day he dies. And the smell. The smell of a garage. Not the garage that sits comfortably within your two-story home, but the garage you pull into, panicked, with a flat tire in the middle of the night. That garage. The one where you think those lying, cheating mechanics work. The one that people bitch about all the time. That's my dad (and three uncles, two cousins, and a dead grandfather). They have those hands.

Below the fingers that pull up his black short sleeve is a tattoo. A tattoo that fills his large bicep. Deep black and red. A melting scroll leads to two bursting red roses, one stacked upon another. I don't know when he got the tattoo; I was too young to remember. The two spots on the scroll once held my name and my mother's name. The tattoo happened, supposedly, during a drunken evening with my mother's two brothers. All three have the same type of tattoo. The ones with the thick green, once black, lines that show the wear of the years. The bold reds and blacks have faded from each man's arm.

J. Wyatt & T. E. Adams (eds.), On (Writing) Families, 37–41.
© *2014 Sense Publishers. All rights reserved.*

Time has changed my father's tattoo in other ways: now it only holds my name. My mother's name is covered in (tattooed) leaves.

But there is one thing that has always bothered me about the tattoo.

I think my name is spelled wrong.

It's difficult to articulate the failure here. The font is script, a jagged rough masculine script, where the letters are pushed close and tight together. It is difficult to make out, and I could be wrong. But, it is my name and I know how my name should look.

My name is Desirée. I see something like Dasirée or maybe Deserée. My name seems blurry, in the photograph and in the flesh. I have never talked to my father about the spelling—I'm too timid to bring it up. Like I said, my father is a big guy. And we have a history together. I am sure he would laugh at me, a hearty laugh that communicates so much. Dismissal. Removal. But I have known this tattooed-name failure for as long as I can remember. What does not asking him about it say about me?

TATTOO AS TEXT

Unless you have a tattoo, and I'm talking about a real tattoo, one with swirls and swishes and lines and edges, you may not know what I mean when I talk about the sound the needle makes when it hits your skin. The unrelenting buzzing marked only through the pain that slowly diminishes with time. Pain that fades, only as pain can, gently into a dull throb. It's a productive pain. The production of this text, that of a tattoo, is one that is built on the foundations of desire buttressed by walls of pain. We all get tattoos for different reasons. But we all started with desire that led to pain.

In this way, the tattoo becomes the text. A text that is living on our bodies that shows our fortitude in the face of that buzzing needle. Whether we were drunk, like my father, or underage, like me–we all have our tattoo stories. We wear them on our bodies proudly (well, some of us do). And, as we age, so does this text. Unlike many other texts, tattoos slide through life with us—the tattoo on a woman's belly swells under the weight of a pregnancy. Or, the person not so different from my father, whose tattoo is spliced with the scars of a life marked by violence.

Our tattoos speak in many different voices and tell many stories. Others have engaged in the autoethnographic (Spry, 2000), ethnographic (Pritchard, 2000), and interpersonal (Doss & Ebesu Hubbard, 2009) explorations of tattoos. But this tattoo, this cacophony of roses mixed with the layers of grime accumulated through countless hours under countless car hoods, is my father. His tattoo is a polysemic text written, with indelible ink, upon his aging bicep.

As a polysemic signifier, my father's tattoo positions him in multiple ways to different people (Ceccarelli, 1998; Dunn, 2011). I'm not interested in rehearsing the negative connotations that are forced upon the bodies of those who fit the preconceived biases of the white working class. In this moment, it hurts my heart to see my father perceived by others through the lens of classist prejudice. That's not what this essay is about. Rather, this tattoo-as-text marks the various ways that the relationships between those with blood ties can fail. This is about our relationship. A relationship that becomes reflected through a tattoo inked on a drunken night in New Jersey.

ON (NOT) TELLING THE STORY

As time weathers our skin, and as the dark black lines become an almost green outline of our past, our memories wear away too. My image of my father in my youth is framed by the very few pictures of my childhood. The important moments. He holds me, as an infant, while he smokes a cigarette and proudly looks into the camera. At 7 I am wearing his sunglasses at the circus. There aren't that many images I have to reference. I rely on the fogginess of my memory and the contradicting stories of my long-divorced parents.

I am not telling the entire story of my relationship with my father because that fogginess has settled into my memories. It's not shame, or embarrassment, or pain that compels my vagueness but a creeping sense that some things are better left unsaid (Goodall, 2000).

There was trouble in my childhood, just like any childhood. I have memories of the police and late-night rides down dark highways towards my grandparents' house. Bruised skin and loud words. There was failure in those places. Failure that changed who he was, who I am, who we are.

SPELLING IS FOR LOSERS

It is important that I attempt to mark the familial entanglements between my father and me as entanglements that I am trying to write through. The polysemic nature of Al's signifying tattoo is my focus, and the (mis)spelling of my name on my own father's bicep helps me to trouble the false narrative of generational continuity that goes (mostly) unspoken within our lives. It took me a long time to realize that I am not my father's daughter. Rather, I am part of a larger community and system of alliances that, yes, include my father but do not start or end with biological family.

The (mis)spelling of my name constitutes a break in the normative frame of the family, a living break that allows me to rethink my relationship with my father through the lens of failure. A break that reappears every time I see him and his arm. As Halberstam (2011) explains about the disavowal of the traditional family, "this queer form of antidevelopment requires healthy doses of forgetting and proceeds by way of a series of substitutions" (p. 73). We have never talked of my

39

perceived misspelling of the tattoo, just as we have never talked about the dark history between us. I remember the tattoo and I remember to forget.

I see the misspelling of the tattoo and I realize that our relationship is built on conversations we will never have. Just as he will probably never read this essay, we will probably never talk about what the misspelling signifies. My name has been on a man's arm for over thirty years and, unlike my mother's name, has never been covered by dark green leaves. My name is allowed through normative forms of understanding to remain on his skin, a "visual text which installs the national narrative as a basis for the personal narrative of marriage and childbearing" (Halberstam, 2011, p. 77). My perception of this misspelling complicates our relationship and his claim to my personhood.

I pause here to mark that I cannot give up my own ability to fail. I might be wrong about the misspelling. It's deeply embedded in my understanding of my father. Our relationship is built on my perceptions of his failure. But I could be the one who is, and has always been, wrong.

Back to theory. Back to forgetting. Back to his claim.

My mother is a small woman. Tiny. I outgrew borrowing my mother's clothes in 7th grade. My father is the big one. My body reflects his and, through this tattoo, his body reflects mine. I see myself in him though I try to reframe our relationship in ways beyond father/daughter. We are bound together by our bodies that are closely matched. His hair, my hair. His fair skin, my fair skin. I work to forget and move forward. The tattoo on his arm reaches towards a constellation of meaning that branches, like a rhizome, into contradictory directions.

There is no easy ending to us.

I see his arm and am amused. Have you figured out why yet? Do we know each other well enough for me to really tell you the truth?

The failure of my father to get the spelling of my name correct in a (permanent) tattoo is a metaphor and a reminder of all the wrongs he committed as a father.

And I know that I should not believe this.

I should be able to complicate my sense-making more.

That's why I rely on Halberstam (2011) to grant me the permission to give up the ghost of the failing father, the deadbeat dad. To move on. To get over it. To push my understandings of what failure is beyond the heteronormative understandings of father. Of what should have been. I am trying to write through my own bias of his failure for me, and to hear the other voices that emerge from his tattoo as text. But, it's hard. Damn hard. I can't keep that from you anymore.

And now I am the one who is failing.

> "The end is the beginning, and yet you go on."
> —Samuel Beckett, *Endgame*

I have a horrible sense of direction, and when I disobey the wishes of the GPS, the feminine voice scolds me with a dry, "recalculating route." She sounds disappointed in me because I went off the path that she so carefully assembled. She knows I should know better and she knows that I always turn south instead of north. She knows that I make mistakes and her voice registers that disappointment. I turn around when possible and make my way, forgetting my mistakes, towards my destination.

The picture of my father's tattoo that hangs in my office reminds me of the possibilities that exist within forgetting and failure. I work to remember the failures. The paths almost taken and the relationships that mark mistakenly travelled relational paths. This forgetting, and remembering, and forgetting again allows for movement within my relationship with my father, a shifting of generational logics that allow me to move through the misspelling of his daughter's name to a place that, each time I see him, allows me to read the text of our relationship again (un)forgetting and (un)remembering just like the first time.

REFERENCES

Beckett, S. (1995). *Nohow on: Company, ill seen ill said, worstward ho: Three novels.* New York: Grove Press.

Beckett, S. (2009). *Endgame and act without words.* New York: Grove Press.

Ceccarelli, L. (1998). Polysemy: Multiple meanings in rhetorical criticism. *Quarterly Journal of Speech, 84,* 395-415.

Doss, K., & Ebesu Hubbard, A. S. (1999). The communicative value of tattoos: The role of public self-consciousness on tattoo visibility. *Communication Research Reports, 26,* 62-74.

Dunn, T. R. (2011). Remembering 'A Great Fag': Visualizing public memory and the construction of queer space. *Quarterly Journal of Speech, 97,* 435-60.

Goodall, Jr. H. L. (2000). *Writing the new ethnography.* New York: AltaMira Press.

Halberstam, J. (2011). *The queer art of failure.* Durham, NC: Duke University Press.

Pritchard, S. (2000). Essence, identity, signature: Tattoos and cultural property. *Social Semiotics, 10,* 331-346.

Spry, T. (2000). Tattoo stories: A postscript to *Skins. Text and Performance Quarterly, 20,* 84-96.

Desirée D. Rowe
Department of Fine Arts and Communication Studies
University of South Carolina Upstate

LIZ BONDI

WHAT'S IN A NAME?

Secrets, Haunting, and Family Ties[1]

"Daddy, what is your middle name?"
"I don't have one."
"Why daddy?"
"Because I don't have one."
"But why?"
"There isn't a reason, I just don't have a middle name."

I was no more than nine years old when this conversation happened and I still cannot say whether my father was telling me the truth or his truth or something else.

My parents had given me and each of my siblings a middle name as well as a first name. Although none of us used our middle names routinely, I grew up very sure that mine belonged to me and when I was asked for my full name, I always included it. I remember too how my mother had a middle name and that she used her middle initial when she wrote her signature. The odd one out in my family was my father who, as I recall, always declared that he had no middle name. But a few months after my ninth birthday any reference to his middle name or its absence was suddenly brought to a halt.

It was the autumn, around the time of my older brother's thirteenth birthday. A parcel arrived addressed to him. It was an unexpected birthday gift from a relative I'd never heard of and whose identity I still do not know. The gift was a book that listed members of my paternal grandmother's family. This version of the book must have been produced soon after my birth because I was included in it along with my two older siblings (first name, middle name, family name for each of us) but my two younger siblings were not listed. I soon came to understand that the gift was probably intended to mark what would have been my brother's *bar mitzvah* had my family observed the custom. It was no secret that my father was Jewish by birth and that my mother was not. Both were avowedly non-religious and brought us up accordingly.

As my memory composes the story, after beginning to explore the book, my older brother was very excited to make a discovery, which he swiftly shared with me and our other siblings (then aged between 5 and 15). The discovery contradicted my father's story about having no middle name: in this book, his first name and his family name appeared just as we already knew them, but sandwiched between, where a middle name should be, was another name, of which we had been ignorant.

J. Wyatt & T. E. Adams (eds.), On (Writing) Families, 43–48.

My siblings and I have different memories of these events, and the variance between them illustrates the fragility and mutability of memory (Loftus, 1996). Shortly before writing this essay, inspired in part by Irene Kacandes' (2009) account of how she began to explore her own and her siblings' memories of learning about their father's boyhood experiences of war, I spoke to each of my siblings on the telephone. Individually, I asked them if they remembered a story about my father's middle name. My older brother, so central to my account, remembered nothing. He didn't contest the story I told, but my telling didn't trigger his own memories. My younger sister, only five at the time, also had no memory of these events. My younger brother remembered the name but thought it was something we children had made up. I assured him that it wasn't made up and that the book existed. I knew this not because I had the book in my possession, but because I was sure that my older sister—the eldest sibling—did. I spoke to her last and her memory of the events I have described thus far is broadly similar to mine, although she recalls my older brother having no interest in the book and that it was she who discovered the previously unknown name. Her account may explain why my older brother did not remember the book or the discovery of the name. If her memory is historically more accurate than mine, my version illustrates something of the compositional work that goes into the construction of memory, in which my sense of the link to my brother, reshaped how I held the story in my mind (Spence, 1982). My memory and my older sister's memory also differ regarding what happened next.

I do not remember how my father became aware of the discovery that one of us had made. Perhaps he witnessed excitement among us and asked us what it was about. Perhaps we went to him to tell him we had discovered that he did after all have a middle name. But however it unfolded, his response tied me into something that I felt to be a secret. I do not recall a clear scene, but I came to believe and "remember" that my father insisted to us that he hated the middle name he had been given, which was why he had denied its existence. Most importantly in my memory, we were sworn to secrecy about it with the utmost seriousness: he told us that we absolutely must remain silent about it henceforth, and must not utter the name anywhere or anytime. My father was not in any sense dictatorial, and he was not a man easily moved to issue threats. But I knew that I had been given an instruction to keep his middle name secret, and that this instruction was uncharacteristically forceful. I had no choice but to treat it seriously. To my nine-year-old self, the message was clear: if I wasn't capable of forgetting the existence of this middle name (which I might speculate two of my siblings succeeded in doing), I must be sure never to utter it. Even now, some 50 years later, and even though I know that the name "escaped" my father's efforts to keep it hidden and can be found on the internet by moderately determined searchers without the book in question, I still feel the weight of that obligation. I do not recall any subsequent conversations with my father (who died in 2005) about the matter.

I am sure that I did have subsequent conversations about the name with my older sister, although not for many years prior to our recent telephone conversation. She did not recall the weighty burden of being sworn to secrecy. Instead she thought that my father had responded by declaring that he knew nothing about the name in question. Her account is entirely plausible. The name that appears in the book between my father's first name and family name is a traditional Hebrew name. It was probably the name by which he would have been called up to the Torah (marking his formal entry into his religious community in his own right) had he been observant. His first name, by which he was always known, is Germanic in origin and was a common name for boys in Austria, where he was born in 1919. It was also common for Jewish parents at this time to give their children a "gentile" as well as a Hebrew name. His parents were not observant Jews and of his mother he wrote that "from early on" she was "a strong rebel against the family orthodoxy and made it clear how much she disliked the narrowness, the self-satisfaction, the blindness of religion" (Bondi, 1990, p. 3). It therefore seems entirely possible that the Hebrew name may not have been given to him by his parents. Perhaps someone in my paternal grandmother's wider family was the source of his Hebrew name, and he never owned it in the way that my siblings, my mother and I each owned our largely unused middle names.

Some light might be shed on the matter of my father's Hebrew name by examining legal papers including his birth certificate, his naturalisation papers, my parents' marriage certificate and Austrian-Jewish records from the period. However my purpose in this essay lies less with the "historical truth" of his name and more with the "narrative truth" of my experience of something secret by which I was bound (Spence, 1982).

In whatever way my father responded to his children's discovery of a Hebrew name attaching to him, I came to feel an imperative to keep the name and its discovery secret. This imperative ties me to my family of origin in a very particular way. There is knowledge about his name that is shared within the family unit but from which others were to be excluded. As was clear, this knowledge also already existed elsewhere in the extended family of which we were a part, but no members of this wider family lived anywhere near us. So my nine-year-old understanding of the secret I was to keep followed precisely the boundary of the family unit that consisted of my parents and my siblings. It reinforced the difference between who and what belonged to my family unit and who and what did not.

Families are, by definition, groups apart, which our modern legal and cultural systems consider to be entitled to at least a degree of privacy. So was my father asking me to keep a secret or to respect something private to our family? The difference between privacy and secrecy is a twentieth century construct now typically understood in terms of the impacts on others of what is held privately or secretly. Keeping a secret implies that something is being concealed that materially affects those excluded from its substance. If secrecy is not intrinsically deleterious, unfair, or unkind, it is nevertheless construed to be the least bad option, which is the typical justification for both state and family secrets (Pulda, 2012). By contrast, privacy protects individuals and families from unwarranted intrusion, and is positively valorised. Privacy enables openness and transparency within its boundaries, benefitting not only those within but also the wider communities to which those families belong.

Much of the damage associated with secrets within families arises from where and how the lines of exclusion are drawn, and therefore who is excluded from knowledge that matters (Pincus & Dare, 1978). Bud Goodall (2005) tells of the toxic consequences of parental secrets from which he was excluded, but which he necessarily bumped up against in the ordinary daily life of his family of origin. After his father died, Goodall discovered layer upon layer of secrecy. The revelation that, for more than two decades, his father had been a spy was just the start of it. Secrets and lies had been his father's trade. His son (an only child) had grown up with a long series of cover stories and a "web of secrecy that finally defined and ensnared us all" (Goodall, 2005, p. 499). Although Goodall (2005) came to "appreciate the delicate balance in my father's decision to not tell me who he really was or what he really did" (p. 510), his account also illustrates how and why "secrecy as a familial strategy [...] is now viewed as destructive, a malign practice that erodes trust, especially between its members" (Cohen, 2013, p. xii).

If my father had attempted to keep a secret from his children about his name, he was rumbled while we were still young. Perhaps, but I am not really sure, he had lied to me when I asked him about his middle name. But was that any more of a lie than the little "white" lies that I was encouraged to tell when I was called upon to be gracious to someone I didn't like? In what sense did it make a difference to me or to anyone if he had concealed a middle name? In no material sense was my trust abused. Once the Hebrew name was out, he did not try to cover it up with lies. Everyone within the family unit knew. There was, therefore, the kind of internal transparency that renders privacy "good." Who was affected, who could be hurt, by the request that we make no further mention of the name within or beyond the family? Perhaps this kind of secret strengthened the bonds of trust within our family rather than eroding them.

But what of my *feeling* of being bound by a secret, which seemed to me to tie my family unit more strongly together? To keep a name secret seems so lacking in substance. Had my father denied his Jewishness, his desire for secrecy about his Hebrew name might have made more sense. But he did not. His Jewishness had always taken a non-religious, highly secularised form, both in the community in which he grew up and in the adult life he made for himself in the United Kingdom. As his mother's attitude to religion indicates, he continued, rather than broke, a family tradition. Growing up in Vienna as Hitler rose to power in Germany and in the context of a pan-German movement, he was certainly subject to anti-Semitism. If he and others around him knew of his Hebrew name back then, I guess it is possible that it was used in anti-Semitic taunts. I might speculate that, for him, the name came to stand for the hatefulness of his exposure to anti-Semitism. When I put to one of my brothers the possibility that this might have motivated my father's desire for the name to be kept secret, his response was "No, that would surely have propelled him in exactly the opposite direction." I think that my brother is right: while I don't recall our father ever speaking explicitly about his childhood experience of anti-Semitism, his lifelong commitment to racial equality, enacted in numerous ways during my childhood, was eloquent evidence of his refusal to collude with such prejudice.

As I mull it over, it makes less and less sense to view my father's Hebrew name as itself a source of shame to be kept secret. The feeling of a secret, one that I can't get rid of, doesn't seem to make sense if it was really about his Hebrew name. Perhaps my feeling of something secret adhering to my father's Hebrew name might be better understood as a sign of the presence of something connected in my mind to my father, but which could not be named, that is something unspeakable, something unthinkable. In this framing I hint towards what French psychoanalyst Nicolas Abraham (1975) has called the "phantom," by which he means "a formation of the unconscious that [...] passes—in a way yet to be determined— from the parent's unconscious to the child's" (p. 173). Lodged inside the child, the phantom "stages the verbal stirrings of a secret buried alive in the [parent's] unconscious" (p. 173). In Abraham's account, which owes much to folklore, "what haunts are not the dead but the gaps left within us by the secrets of others" (p. 171). Perhaps I came to be haunted by "a secret buried alive" (p. 173) within my father's unconscious of which he was wholly unaware. Maybe this phantom came to him from his own parents, maybe from within his own life, but something shameful, unspeakable, traumatic.

The idea of unconscious transmission from one generation to the next is central to psychoanalytic thinking: our earliest relationships shape our identities and the past is always alive in the present. The Scottish psychoanalyst W.R.D. Fairbairn (1952) reformulated Freud's thinking on the forces that shape the emerging infant psyche, and suggested that our complex sense of ourselves is forged through the inevitable traumas of infant helplessness and dependency on fallible, imperfect parents. Reflecting on Freud's preoccupation with Jewish identity in writings from the last decade of his life, Stephen Frosh (2013) asks if "we might have to see all identity construction as a mode of traumatic possession" (p. 120). He continues "[h]aunting is then the *norm*, not the pathological exception" (p. 120, emphasis in original). On this account our identities are constituted by the very gaps and secrets that haunt us.

My sense of being bound by a family secret tells a narrative truth that does not align easily with a historical truth. When I explore my memories and those of which my siblings speak, attempting to find or to forge some narrative coherence, my father's apparent secrecy about his Hebrew name makes less and less sense. And yet the feeling of secrecy persists and somehow seems woven in to my relationship with my father when he was alive and since he died. It tells me something about who I am, keeping alive in me my sense of belonging to my family of origin, not just in name, but in the fabric of who I am. It seems integral to my identity, not as a pathological inheritance, but in the most ordinary sense of a family tie.

NOTES

[1] I would like to thank my siblings whose conversations with me made this essay possible and whose generous responses to an earlier draft helped to shape it. I would like to also thank Judith Fewell, Phillip Jurczyk, Tony Adams, and Jonathan Wyatt for feedback on an earlier draft.

REFERENCES

Abraham, N. (1975). Notes on the phantom: A complement to Freud's metapsychology. In N. Abraham & M. Torok (Eds.), *The shell and the kernel* (N. T. Rand, Trans., pp. 171-176). Chicago: University of Chicago Press.

Bondi, H. (1990). *Science, Churchill and me*. Oxford: Pergamon Press.

Cohen, D. (2013). *Family secrets*. London: Penguin.

Fairbairn, W. R. D. (1952). *Psychoanalytic studies of the personality*. London: Routledge & Kegan Paul.

Frosh, S. (2013). *Hauntings: Psychoanalysis and ghostly transmissions*. New York: Palgrave Macmillan.

Goodall, H. L. Jr. (2005). Narrative inheritance: A nuclear family with toxic secrets. *Qualitative Inquiry, 11*, 492-513.

Kacandes, I. (2009). *Daddy's war*. Lincoln: University of Nebraska Press.

Loftus, E. (1996). *Eyewitness testimony*. Cambridge, MA: Harvard University Press.

Pincus, L. & Dare, C. (1978). *Secrets in the family*. London: Faber.

Pulda, M. (2012). Unknown knowns: State secrets and family secrets. *Biography, 35*, 472-491.

Spence, D. (1982). *Narrative truth and historical truth: Meaning and interpretation in psychoanalysis*. New York: W. W. Norton.

Liz Bondi
Counselling and Psychotherapy
The University of Edinburgh

MARK FREEMAN

FROM ABSENCE TO PRESENCE

Finding Mother, Ever Again

As a long-time student of memory and identity as well as the son of a 90-year old woman with dementia, I have had a remarkable opportunity to try to understand and narrate the trajectory of her experience. The process has been difficult. The fact that she is my mother, and has suffered, is one reason. Another is the fact that much of her experience remains obscure, such that I can only surmise the realities of her inner world. In addition, there is the challenge of narrative itself, that is, of finding a way to tell her story—which is, in part, mine as well—that truly does justice to her life. That much of her story has been tragic is clear enough. I won't be skating over these periods; they were extremely painful for her and for those of us who had been entrusted with her care, so much so that we could sometimes lose sight of her "face," as Levinas (1985, 1999) refers to it, her existence as another, worthy and in need. But nor will I focus on these alone. For there have been other periods, and other dimensions of relationship, that have been quite beautiful–and that could not have emerged without her very affliction. This is part of the story too. So it is that I have come to think of her story as a kind of "tragicomedy," one that is emblematic of nothing less than life itself.

I

Had I been given the opportunity to reflect on the challenges of writing about my mother's situation two or three years ago, this "meditation" would have been entirely different. Indeed, it wouldn't have *been* a "meditation," but rather more like a lamentation or, depending on the moment, an outright rant. That is because her situation at the time was awful, and whatever "light" may have emerged at the time—and there was some—was overwhelmed by the darkness, even the horror, of what had been going on. Needless to say, there are still some very tough times: Mom still has dementia; she has Chronic Obstructive Pulmonary Disease (COPD); she is confined to a wheelchair most of the time; and she can hardly see. Most of her teeth are missing (she has had two "partials" that have managed to disappear over the past year or so), her arms and hands are all red and blue because her skin is so paper-thin that she bruises easily, and, when I enter the common room to see her, she will more than likely be slumped over, eyes closed, maybe dozing, but possibly just … being. So, it's hardly a rosy picture. But things are different now – she is different as am I—and it has led me to want to tell her story in a different way than I would have, than I *did*, back then.

J. Wyatt & T. E. Adams (eds.), On (Writing) Families, 49–55.

Bearing this narrative turnabout in mind, it may be useful for me briefly to recount the few pieces I have written about her. In some important respects, they trace the chapters of her life since the time of her diagnosis some seven years ago. The first, called "Beyond Narrative: Dementia's Tragic Promise" (2008a), essentially described the earliest phases, when she had some awareness of her own undoing, and had protested mightily, and often loudly, against it. There wasn't much comedy back then. Here was a woman who not too long ago had driven a car, managed her checkbook, did her own taxes, and much more, who was suddenly losing it. To make matters worse, she would often *forget* the very history within which we had all become enmeshed. She had been put into assisted living against her will, or so she believed; things were being stolen from her, she believed; and I, of course, living just a couple miles away, was the primary villain. "You're treating me like a child," she would sometimes say.

These were tough times. And if truth be told, I sometimes wasn't at my best back then. Her incessant repetition of questions could be annoying. Her refusals to believe the truth—for instance, that she had hidden things away only to have become convinced that they had been taken from her (most likely by the help, of course)—were frustrating. And her accusations, especially those having to do with the (alleged) fact that my brothers and I had placed her in assisted living against her will (she was fully in on the decision but had no memory of it and consequently felt that it had been done behind her back), that none of us wanted her (she had insisted years ago that she would never want to move in with us), that I never came to see her (I went to see her multiple times per week) and so on, could be downright maddening—and this, of course, despite the fact that she was utterly helpless to do anything but exactly what she was doing. So there I was getting angry at my failing, demented mother for doing things she couldn't possibly help doing. What a sensitive son!

Levinas has spoken of our being "hostage" to the face of the Other, captivated by its very presence, its nakedness and need. "It is through the condition of being a hostage that there can be pity, compassion, pardon, and proximity in the world— even the little there is, even the simple 'after you sir'" (1996, p. 91). I was a hostage all right, but to my own rather primitive emotions more than anything else. The result was that *she*—my mother, this tormented and confused person, feeling herself coming undone, holding onto what she could—was sometimes barely visible. Her face was all but absent, and in its place would be my own projections, my own wishes and needs. It wasn't always like this; I was present to her, and she to me, plenty of the time. But I look back humbly on this inaugural period. It was painful and difficult to see her so compromised, and, as I can see now, I did some serious protesting of my own.

But I also began to see a correlation of sorts back then, one that in its own tragic way promised a measure of reprieve, for my mother as well as for me: the more her ego was on the line—the more, for instance, her autonomy and self-sufficiency were cast into question, whether by people or by situations—the more she would suffer; and the more her ego was in abeyance—listening to some music at a summer concert, having a glass of wine or a gin and tonic—the more comfortable and happy she would be. It was around this time that I realized that as her dementia progressed and her self-consciousness, in turn, diminished she would likely be "better off," at least subjectively. I even flirted with the idea that with the continued loss of her ego, she might attain something akin to mystical union, her very "unself," as Iris Murdoch (1970) might put it, leading to a kind of ecstatic connection to the world. Hence the idea of dementia's "tragic promise": owing to her continuing demise, she would have an unprecedented opportunity to be truly present to reality. It would be a quite different path to the kind of selflessness frequently associated with meditation, mindfulness practices, and so on—a kind of crash course, you could say—but it would be no less ecstatic for all that. Or so it seemed.

II

Even then I knew that it would be a challenge to tell her story. Part of what was going on was tragic, to be sure. But part of it was also beautiful in a way. In a second piece I did, called "Life without Narrative? Autobiography, Dementia, and the nature of the Real" (2008b), I even told a story of how, one fall day, as mom and I were on a country drive up a nearby mountain, she had been so completely enraptured with the world that, for a moment or two (no longer, I assured the reader), I envied her. In a very real sense, she was utterly and completely care-free. I was into it too; it was a gorgeous New England day, multicolored leaves were all around, there were incredible vistas, and I was glad to be there, with her. But I was also acutely aware of the circumstances, and I still had all kinds of clutter in my mind, miscellaneous stuff that would surge in and bring me back inside myself, to this or that task or concern. In meditative practice, this cluttered state is sometimes referred to as "monkeymind," our thoughts swinging from branch to branch. That particular day, I wished I could have been a bit more like mom, at least in this one way. (What a strange wish.)

Whatever envy I might have had was cast aside later that year. For, instead of this seemingly selfless state of carefree abandon, my mother would frequently experience a kind of existential "dislocation," such that everything would become utterly alien to her. Waking up in the morning, she was generally okay; the routines began and she could make her way through them without getting too disturbed. But she would sometimes wake up after an afternoon nap only to find herself completely lost, scared and panicky. It was around this time that I would sometimes get a call at work. She had to speak to me, now. Or I had to drive over to see her, be there in the flesh. "I don't know where I am. I don't know *who* I am," she had said. Nobody at her assisted living place could say or do anything to bring her down. How could they? She didn't recognize any of them. What's more, "They don't know what's going on here." Her confusion became their ignorance and incompetence. It could get even more severe, though. "There's no one around, not a person," she complained to me one time. "There *are* people around," I told her. "So, why am I so completely alone here now, so completely lost?" Not an easy question to answer.

51

I learned some important things around this time. For one, I learned that the complete or near-complete dissolution of the self, far from leading to mystical transport, led instead to the void. I also learned that even though "life itself" may not be quite as narrative-laden as some theorists (including me) have suggested, life *without* narrative, without some sense of location and rootedness in one's history and story, could be horrifying. "Presence"—my presence—was nothing short of a lifeline for my mother those days. At times, I was her sole connection to reality, and she would cling to me for dear life. Leaving to go home or back to work has always been difficult, but it was extra difficult during this phase. On a good day, I'm sure it didn't matter much: out of sight, out of mind. But I have no doubt that on other days, she would feel abandoned and alone again, without any touchstones, any meaningful connections to the world. I shudder to think about it, even now.

III

The next piece I did, entitled "The Stubborn Myth of Identity: Dementia, Memory, and the Narrative Unconscious" (2009), brought me back to a somewhat more upbeat story, and for at least two reasons. First, just when I had begun to assume that my mother was about ready to "exit" completely—by which I mean leave her identity and sense of self completely behind—she re-emerged, in a way. It wasn't pretty, mind you; she would sometimes speak of being "brainless," "mindless," "like a child." Her identity, in other words, such as it was, had largely become a negative one, tied to what she no longer was. This was a tough period too. There was no longer the kind of protest there had been earlier; there was confusion and lamentation and mourning, over what had clearly, and irrevocably, been lost. What was amazing was that, through it all, "she"—my mother—was still there. There could even be moments of empathy on her part: "What you must feel like when you leave, to see your poor mother like this." She would often utter some words in Yiddish, which translate roughly as "Oh, what a person becomes." And in those moments when she had some fleeting insight into her own sorry state, she would add "Oh, my God. Oh, my God."

As I noted in a subsequent piece, called "Narrative Foreclosure in Later Life: Possibilities and Limits" (2010), she had become relatively devoid of deep feeling about her situation at this juncture. "She doesn't cry, which she did in the past," I noted; "her response is more cerebral, even intellectual. It also doesn't seem particularly personal; there is loss, to be sure, but it's not so much 'hers' as it is an awareness of human loss, human demise, the fate of people and their stories. There is still some sense of identity, but it is highly diffuse, even, strangely enough, impersonal .... Even now," I went on to say, "there is an image in view of who and what she once was. But unlike the earlier years, when she would fight mightily to hold onto this image, there's no holding on anymore. She no longer knows 'the story.' But she does seem to know that it's over" (p. 17). This is essentially what I meant by the idea of "narrative foreclosure."

Was there anything to be done about it? Was there anything I could say to her that might allow her to open up her story once again and to live with some measure of hope? "Strictly speaking," I wrote, "I think the answer is 'no.'" Why? "Given that she has only the most minimal sense of the future, it's hard to imagine what it is that she might live *for*, if by 'for' we are referring to some purpose, some motivating source of meaning and value" (2010, p. 18). Put in the simplest of terms, my mother's situation was, and remains … hopeless. How could it be otherwise? How strange it is that she and I, together, have so much to share.

IV

The good news? Or, more appropriately, the bad/good news? Most of what I have been considering throughout these pages has passed. Owing to the progression of her disease, my mother is well beyond the kind of panic and terror I described earlier, and, as far as I can tell, well beyond feeling abandoned. She's still sometimes confused when I leave, but in a much less anxious way. "Going home, ma; got to get some dinner." "Oh, okay." I hustle out, quickly. And within what's probably a matter of seconds, I'm gone from her world: out of sight, out of mind.

Right now, my mother really has no idea at all where she is. "Whose place is this?" she'll ask. Or: "Do *you* live here?" The weird thing is, that's just fine at this point. In fact, she and I will sometimes sit in her room—her "apartment," as I usually refer to it—and she'll say, "This is a *lovely* place." "It is, isn't it," I might respond, "It's lucky we found it." Objectively speaking, it's really not all that lovely; it's a nice, competently run institution, no more, no less. Seen from the outside, her situation remains bleak. The disease has intensified, and has left her in a state of dependency and vulnerability and fragility that would have once horrified her. She needs to be taken to the bathroom now. She needs to be dressed. She needs to be fed. The fact is, there's very little she can do on her own. But I would no longer describe her situation as "tragic"—not primarily so, anyway.

On any given day, I can walk into the dayroom, where people sit, watch TV (or look in its direction), have snacks, and carry out simple activities. And there she'll be, just like I described before, slumped over, eyes closed, maybe dozing, maybe not; it's hard to tell. I walk over and play with her hair a little without saying a word. If all goes well, her eyes will crawl open and she'll smile a gap-toothed smile. "Hi, honey," she might say. If she doesn't respond, I might ask, "Anybody home?" Then, hopefully, she'll know I'm there. "How did you find me?" she may ask. "I always find you, ma. Should we take a little spin?" And then we'll go to her room or, if it's a nice day, go outside, take a wheel through the parking lot or sit by a nice little garden, and try to catch up as best we can. If it's one of her good days, she might cry out "Wheeeee!!!" as we roll along, like a little kid. There will be pleasure when she feels the sun hit her face.

She might go on to ask questions about me and my life—what I do for a living, whether I'm married, whether we have any kids. Sometimes she knows all of this, but generally not. One way or the other, there's always some measure of re-acquaintance needed. It can be hard. In one recent exchange, this re-acquaintance process took some time. "So, you're my son?" she asked after I identified myself. "Are you married? Do you have any children?" I answer. "And what is your name?" Eventually, there were more questions: "So, do you like me as a mother?" "So, how long have I been your mother?" "57 years." "That's a long time not to know you." She asks the same question again, and I answer again. "Wow. Look at all the time I've missed with you," she says this time. "So, do you call me 'ma'?" "So, when did I get to know you?" "So, are you nice?" "So, do I look at you with love?" By the end of this rather strange exchange, a few more precious words are shared. "I love being your mom," she said. "I love being your son," I replied. "So," she concluded, "it's a good match." And then silence, being-with, presence.

I see the time I have with my mother as a gift. And on some level, she seems to feel the same. Even when she doesn't quite know who I am, or who she is, or where she is, our being together seems reassuring and right. "What am I to you?" she asked during another recent visit. "Your brother? Son?" "You mean what am *I* to *you*," I explain. "I'm your son." "Mark?" she asks. "You know who I am! Why else would you call me 'honey'?" (which she had done a few moments before). "Because I love you," she says. More silence. I rub her arm or run my fingers through her hair. Or we just sit together, feeling what we can. I look at her; I see her face. She gazes ahead; there's a very faint smile. At this particular moment, she seems grateful and glad to be alive. I am too.

V

I have only begun to tell my mother's story—which, again, is not hers alone but mine as well. I earlier referred to this story as a "tragicomedy," and my aim is to tell it in its full measure. What might this mean?

First, and most importantly: My aim is to tell it in all of its dimensions, from the tragic and horrifying all the way to the comic and redemptive. This aspect, the *phenomenological*, is primary. In speaking of my aim of telling her story in its full measure, therefore, I am speaking not of offering some sort of definitive, exhaustive account but one that is adequate to the full range of her experience.

Second, I want it to be mainly about her, *her* world. This doesn't mean that I want to leave myself entirely out of the picture; I couldn't even if I wanted to. But one of the things I've learned through the years is how important it is to bracket my view of things and to simply see, and respect, hers. I might wish that she could see better. Or that she was more active. Or that she cared when I wasn't there. I might wish, in other words, that she still had an existence more like my own. But she doesn't. And it's important, I think, to preserve her in her difference, her otherness, her own unique integrity. In this respect, one might say that there's an *anthropological* aspect to writing her story too. I want to enter this native realm as best I can.

Third, even as I want to tell her story in its difference, its otherness, I also want to tell it in its essential humanness. She is not an alien being; she's a *human* being, who, even amidst her myriad maladies and infirmities and occasional oddities, shows wonderfully human traits: humor, compassion, care, love. I want to be sure to keep these qualities visible. We might think of this as the *ethical* aspect of telling her story.

Fourth and finally, I want to tell her story in a way that allows her to truly "live on the page." This is the *aesthetic* aspect of the endeavor. I'm not referring here to embellishment or ornamentation—to somehow "dressing up" her story. I'm speaking instead of the profound challenge of finding language, finding words, that open up the reality and the truth of her existence. From one angle, the project is a "scientific" one, my aim being to practice fidelity to the realities at hand. From another, it's an "artistic" or "poetic" one, my aim being to create a picture, a portrait, that lives and breathes and that somehow discloses her world. Writing the tragicomedy of dementia thus leads me to what I've referred to elsewhere (e.g., Freeman, 2011) as "poetic science." It's an extraordinary challenge and opportunity.

REFERENCES

Freeman, M. (2008a). Beyond narrative: Dementia's tragic promise. In L-C. Hyden & J. Brockmeier (Eds.), *Health, illness, and culture: Broken narratives* (pp. 169-184). London: Routledge.

Freeman, M. (2008b). Life without narrative? Autobiography, dementia, and the nature of the real. In G.O. Mazur (Ed.), *Thirty year commemoration to the life of A.R. Luria* (pp. 129-144). New York: Semenko Foundation.

Freeman, M. (2009). The stubborn myth of identity: Dementia, memory, and the narrative unconscious. *Journal of Family Life, 1*. Retrieved March 19, 2009 from http://www.journaloffamilylife.org/mythofidentity.html

Freeman, M. (2010). Narrative foreclosure in later life: Possibilities and limits. In G. Kenyon, E. Bohlmeijer, & W. Randall (Eds.), *Storying later life: Issues, investigations, and interventions in narrative gerontology* (pp. 3-19). New York: Oxford University Press.

Freeman, M. (2011). Toward poetic science. *Integrative Psychological and Behavioral Science, 45,* 389-396

Levinas, E. (1985). *Ethics and infinity*. Pittsburgh, PA: Duquesne University Press.

Levinas, E. (1996). Substitution. In A. T. Peperzak, S. Critchley, & R. Bernasconi (Eds.), *Emmanuel Levinas: Basic philosophical writings* (pp. 80-95).

Bloomington, IN: Indiana University Press. (Original work published 1968)

Levinas, E. (1999). *Alterity and transcendence*. New York: Columbia University Press.

Murdoch, I. (1970). *The sovereignty of good*. London: Routledge.

Mark Freeman
Department of Psychology
College of the Holy Cross

BEATRICE ALLEGRANTI

CORPOREAL KINSHIP

Dancing the Entanglements of Love and Loss

Drawing from personal experience of loss following the death of my mother (Allegranti, 2005, 2011; Allegranti & Wyatt, 2013), this chapter explores how the entanglements of losing and loving are inevitable corporeal processes of kinship: a material discursive co-implication of biological and lived intersubjectivity "intra-acting"[1] (Barad, 2007) over intergenerational time.

The chapter emerges from working in a multi-modal way with four entangled (Barad, 2007) layers: (i) felt-sense movement improvisation (Allegranti, 2011); (ii) writing; (iii) verbal processing; (iv) witnessing. My writing weaves between autobiographical written and danced accounts as well as responses from an invited witness.[2] In so doing, I attempt to engage with the relation between material and discursive phenomena in order to privilege neither bodies nor language in oppositional hierarchy (Barad, 2007).

Building on the feminist poststructuralist work of Judith Butler (2004, 2006), the materialist posthumanism of Karen Barad (2007), the phenomenological work of Elizabeth Grosz (2005), and Anne Fausto-Sterling's biological framework (2000), I consider how embodied personal and social politics shape our human development and contribute to the construction of our psychophysical and ethical selves. I also consider how this embodiment influences our ongoing capacity for *doing* corporeal love and loss as well as how attention to the body problematizes the great "master" discourse of kinship and mortality.

BIRTHDAY (2013)

I dreamt of you last night. You often appear in my dreams on significant dates. We were in a dance school and you were going to a class. I said I'd meet you afterwards and we could go and celebrate your special day—your arrival into the world. This thought now tugs at my longing. I remember when I took you to the South Bank on your birthday to hear Isabel Allende speak about her daughter's death (Allende, 2000). When describing this profound loss she said simply, "It's an inconvenience—not being able to go out shopping and have coffee with her." I knew immediately. It's the everyday being-together activities that make up a life, and a loving-in-action. Today I miss you more. Your absence matters in a way that is incomprehensibly inarticulable (Allegranti & Wyatt, 2013). And yet, my dreaming body is fluent (Mindell, 1987).

J. Wyatt & T. E. Adams (eds.), On (Writing) Families, 57–67.

*

Thinking beyond the poststructural emphasis on "I" being solely discursively constructed, Fausto-Sterling (2000) reminds us how we "incorporate experience into our very flesh" (p. 20). Also, having an understanding that our bodies develop in relationship with other bodies re-frames humanist understandings of the self/body as a bounded stable entity: bodies are co-created and porous and we do not inhabit ourselves by ourselves—we are constantly undone and remade (Allegranti, 2011; Butler, 2004).

I am struck by the paradox of birthday: celebration (at best) and a temporal mourning. In response to this, with pen in hand, I invoke one hundred years of solitude (Marquez, 2007) by mistakenly writing 1913 at the top of my journal entry. I am immediately drawn to Grosz's (2005) understanding of time and space as "active ingredients in the making of matter, and thus in the constitution of objects and subjects" (pp. 173-74). What do I re-constitute in *this* space-time, in the dance studio, with my witness? What materializes in my movement? How can I reconstitute myself in the absence of my maternal presence through the materiality of moving? Can there be a corporeal reclaiming after loss? Young (2005) reminds me that "(e)veryone is born in loss. Ejected from the dark comfort of the mother's body, we are thrown into a world without walls, with no foundation to our fragile and open-ended existence" (p. 128). After moving I reflect on my corporeal forming of *Birthday*:

Undoing, tears, sobs. Where are you? I can't see you. I can't hear you. I can't feel you. Longing to touch you. Are you there? In my body? I keep you close. Child's arms reaching to be held. Nurtured. I can't leave the floor. I need to feel my weight on the floor. Solid. Grounding. Sighing. Breath. (Un)folding rhythm: you are there beside me but I can't stop the tears.

*

Young (2005) astutely observes that "The most primordial intentional act is the motion of the body orienting itself with respect to and moving within its surroundings" (p. 35). Early developmental processes are foundational and diffractive—development unfolds in a dynamic system of overlapping cycles of learning in which we can consider our bodies changing over time within a network of developmental resources, e.g. genes, parents, environment (Fausto-Sterling, 2000; Oyama, 2000). But what kind of (adult) developmental stage is mourning? Understanding the foundational quality of my developmental experience helps me to write and move both my mother and me—into existence. My ontogenetic body bears my mother's imprint and, through movement improvisation, I engage my somatic sensorial attention through sight, touch, sound, and hearing, and I am able to bring awareness to my own developmental processes. In this sense I am, as Sheets-Johnstone (2000) writes, "apprentice" of my corporeal-kinetic body, learning my body and learning to move myself into life after loss.

Inside of You

Acknowledging the fluidity of environment, identities, and history, Young (2005) writes that "stories must be told and retold to each new generation to keep a living, meaningful history" (p. 143). These stories are embodied in our memories, emotions, and psychophysical selves, and as I move, without plan, not knowing by what I am seized (Butler, 2004), my witness provides felt-sense and multisensory kinesthetic responses that shift beyond an emphasis on visual representation into an *intra*-corporeal engagement (Allegranti & Wyatt, 2013). Our intra-actions produce a series of embodied "I"s, resulting in embodied performances that are multilayered: autobiographical, relational, and political (Allegranti, 2011). My embodied performance in *Birthday* prompted my witness to experience a shifting presence-absence between my body and my mother's body:

> *I see someone asleep. Sleep searching. Your hands are over your eyes and I don't know if you want to see her. You definitely want to feel her and you want to hear her. That's what I see in terms of your searching. Your searching body. And then, the story changes, your story changes, and you try to find her in you. In your body, in your core. In every inch of you. In all the cells. Inside of you. And then, a pause. And there's something about that pause that is accepting, whatever that means. But you've got your hand out, ready.*

In this autobiographical unfolding it is not that I do not want to see her— *I cannot*—not only in the material sense, but I cannot fully capture what it is *in* my mother that I have lost (Butler, 2004). In this way, my grief contains the "possibility of apprehending a mode of dispossession that is fundamental to who I am" (Butler, 2006, p. 28). Perhaps this is the "acceptance" that was witnessed in my movement—there is an afterlife in my outstretched hand and

I come to "accept" the material composition of who I am after losing my mother. This ontogenetic exploration led me to understand the ways in which transitions can be possible in the intersubjective process of finding her-in-me and me-in-her.

Yet this is a paradox, my hand is out, ready. Butler (2006) is aware of this incorporation too: "I think I have lost 'you' only to discover that 'I' have gone missing as well" (p. 22). Butler goes on to explain:

> perhaps what I have lost "in" you, that for which I have no ready vocabulary, is a relationality that is composed neither exclusively of myself nor you, but is to be conceived as *the tie* by which those terms are differentiated and related. (p. 22)

Is this the precariousness of life to which Butler (2006) attests? Loss is invariably part of our intersubjective reality, and our precariousness seems to be played out especially when experiencing the death of a loved one. Loss can be a time of emotional crisis akin to early developmental experiences when the baby's body may not be received or met. Notwithstanding the gendered significance of early developmental embodiment between mother and baby, when my mother died there was no longer *mutual* recognition, and yet I continue to seek this recognition since it is an experience that is part of my psychophysical being-in-the-world.

PASSPORT (1944)

Her mother dead for over a year, a nineteen-year old woman gives birth to a girl. The young woman is unmarried. Promises—from the older, professionally established friend of the family and father of her baby—immaterialise. She is left with this shame in a rural, Catholic and conservative Ireland of its time. Her sister, who is married and already has three children, takes the baby in and raises her. Nothing will be said to this child about her biological mother. Nothing that is, until one day on her eighteenth birthday she wants a passport; she has a strong desire to leave this stifling land, this family with its confusing, oppressive and secretive attachments. Then, she discovers the truth from her "sister": "you're not one of us."

*

In telling this story, I trespass into a labyrinth and stumble upon a taboo. Trevarthen (2004) writes that "the baby's signs of unhappiness or 'shame' when there is a chance that he or she will not be understood or liked are emotions that guide our sympathies and growth of self confidence throughout life" (pp. 2-3). Although a useful emotion for babies to learn for later social negotiation, for my mother this sense of shame was politically layered and resulted in her being dispossessed of her kinship (Butler, 2006). In spite of this, during my own childhood I experienced a "good enough" holding (Winnicott, 1971).

However, it is not possible to locate corporeal vulnerability and mourning without entering the sphere of politics (Butler, 2006). Dominant discourses view kinship as dualistic, and hence, there is an implicit humanist understanding of subjectivity—as if a biological tie is a good predictor for lasting commitment or the absence of a biological tie a predictor for the instability of commitment (Alcoff, 2012). My mother experienced a material tie not only to her biological parents but, with her aunt, uncle and cousins; those who provided close physical proximity—an extra-biological emotional relation. And yet, despite the cultural revolutions (in some parts of the world), the patrilineal, heterosexual, and biological kinship system continues to exile lesbian and gay families.

From a materialist perspective, nature and culture are inseperable. And, crucially, language and bodies are not neutral: We are not blank slates awaiting socio-cultural inscription. Bodies *become* sexed and gendered through a mutually influencing process of biological and social construction that evolves over time. Our sexed and gendered experiences are adaptive and shape our flesh constructing our anatomy over time. This merging of biology and culture has implications for how we understand our (cognitive and physical) health—how we "do" our lives.

What, then, are the entangled boundaries of bodies and kinship—if, for example, we consider the intermeshed corporeality of surrogate mothers or in vitro fertilization? Or the entangled boundaries of mothers who do not bond with their daughters or mothers who are not "permitted" to bond with their daughters? In a Foucauldian (1991) sense, state governance of bodies has never seemed clearer than with the Irish Magdalene Asylums of the 18th to 20th centuries, where love, female sexuality, and loss were regulated, punished, and forbidden (Finnegan, 2001). In such cases, embodied selves leak out beyond the discursive confines of birth certificates and passports.

BEATRICE ALLEGRANTI

For Women

No. No. No. No. No. No. NO.
Injustice.
Coercion.
Rape.
Rejection.
Struggle, thrashing, weighty, kicking, stamping. I fall.
NO! I slam against the door. My body is pulsating.
I struggle with the handle—pushing and pulling, trying to get out. Locked in.
Trapped.
Imprisoned. Holding on. I'll hold on forever. I'll never let go. When is it time to let
go? I fall backwards, release my weight into the smooth grey floor, uncurl one
vertebra at a time and softly walk away. Leave through another way: an open
window.

*

We carry our ancestral, genetic line, other bodies, other stories, in our body. What then am I re-storying here in in my movement practice and in this writing? Young (2005) reminds us that,

> the narratives of the history of what brought us here are not fixed, and part of
> the creative and moral task of preservation is to reconstruct the connection of
> the past to the present in light of new events, relationships, and political
> understandings. (p. 144)

How, then, can I become other than who I was before this loss (White, 2000)?

We are ancient when we're born and our body stories are told and retold in the phenomenological structure of everyday life (and in the psychotherapeutic relationship). My own ontogenetic movement exploration of *Passport* transports (Leahy, O'Dwyer & Ryan, 2012) me in my understanding of being a daughter and a woman, and my witness draws attention to the gendered nature of my improvisation:

> *I had a sense of you doing that dance, that whole dance for you, for your*
> *mum and for women, as a collective, doing it for us all.*

In this embodied performance, I am haunted by the ghosts of matrilineal demons and pulled to consider my material choices in terms of sexuality, gender, and reproductive rights. This seems particularly poignant in light of reproductive restrictions for women in Ireland in the past and even today. Sex, gender, and kinship are ensnarled in cultural and historical understandings that reinforce binary categories of male/female and their different phenomenological experience of embodiment. And yet, women and men continue to experience a differential relationship to the *possibility* of reproduction, regardless of whether reproduction becomes a reality (Alcoff, 2012).

62

In movement, I played with these corporeal markers of social flesh. With the materiality of the locked door, the door handle, the grey floor, the open window— all these became transitional objects that I experienced both internally and externally (Winnicott, 1971). The tone of my vocal "NO!" was sourced from the felt sense (Gendlin, 1996) and increased in volume with each repetition. My languaging of this experience also became a movement response shifting beyond representation—since I speak *from* the body.

CAPOEIRA (2003)

You visit my Capoeira[3] class on this bright January morning—your birthday. I look at your face and can see that although there is wonder in those beautiful aquamarine eyes there are moments when you draw a breath, cautious for your daughter's safety as she develops the disciplinary regime (Foucault, 1991) of this improvisational and acrobatic form. As I turn and interweave with another and move in response to the rhythm of the Birembau[4]—I feel strong. I say to you later, "I feel so strong—as though I could cope with anything." After, we talk with my Mestre[5] and his mother who is visiting from Brazil. I am preparing to visit his hometown and our school in Guaratinguetá, he tells you of the beautiful gardens with monkeys in the trees. I don't know at this point that I won't make it to Brazil at this time. We don't know at this point that you are dying. That you will have taken your last breath nine weeks later, the day before mother's day.

*

There is kinesthetic intelligence in the improvisational dyadic exchange in capoeira. Movers do not engage with a known, predetermined destination, but rather we unfold, constantly re-forming: our intra-actions create this *jogo*.[6] I have grown another body through this technology of the self (Foucault, 1988), a body after loss, and, I am moved in more ways than one. Capoeira has shaped my neurocognitive, perceptual and physiological development in a profound way, and the corporeal re-forming has been subtle and time-layered and within a supportive and cultural system (Oyama, 2000). Selves are intersubjectively constituted in the kinesthetic *doing* of capoeira.

Through my movement capacity in capoeira I am in touch with my body's agency, my aliveness. By stretching my ability to improvise, to respond quickly, to make corporeal decisions about attack and defense, I face the limits of my "identity": shame, inhibition, fear of injury, weakness, and a tendency to grow tense in a confrontation (Downey, 2005). I am ever mindful of this Afro-Brazilian aesthetic in a White-dominated society (Downey, 2005), and yet, I experience that difference as always in motion. There are multiple identity shifts in this improvisational exchange acting as a constant reminder that body boundaries are fluid. Boundaries are entangled between the other and me; my Irish-Italian self; English and Portuguese languages; and the body politics of race, gender, sexuality, age, and class.

63

Capoeira presents a constantly changing set of vulnerabilities—something my mother must have seen with her maternal gaze. In capoeira, vulnerability is described as "being open" (Downey, 2005, p. 138) and, I seem to have spent a lifetime re-learning when to open and close my body according to the relational moment through readjusting and self-monitoring rather than repeating. This corporeal vulnerability emerges during my movement practice:

Ouch. Bang. Queda de rins.[7] It feels as though I'm breathing for both of us as I shift my weight around the studio, skin, and, at times, touching the smooth grey dance floor and, at other times, defying gravity. My body is open—I remember to protect and quickly fold my limbs inward towards my core. After a decade of capoeira the connection I have with this movement practice is rooted in my becoming other. Another without you, my roots. Every interaction and inversion that I experience is a connection with you. It's the freedom of having loved. Still loving as I fall.

This corporeal ontology calls individualism—that great master discourse of "I" — into question. We are processual beings, unbound—in a way that draws attention to Butler's (2010) sense that "the body does not belong to itself" (pp. 52-53). Where do I end and you begin during this entangled movement exchange? This dyadic form offers material support in re-corporalising my identity. As Mestre Acordeon writes, "Capoeria is not an outfit that we wear in certain moments of for special occasions. Capoeira is our own skin. It is with us at every moment" (cited in Downey, 2005, p. 23). The materiality of movement in capoeira allows me to experience an "I" that never stands still, that is unknowing (though not epistemologically so), since our bodily self-perception is formed on the basis of past information—which is always out of date with our current physical body (Fausto-Sterling, 2000). And yet, for what does the *not-knowing* allow?

Not-Knowing

Between the two players and the *roda*[8] of bodies that surround us, I wonder what Winnicott (1971) would have made of this holding environment? A human and non-human circle of movement where imagined and historical narratives, past and present, are mobilized in song and music, and, in turn, produce an experiential space for the pair to play in the center.

This kinesthetic intersubjectivity is lived with others in a diversity of ways contingent upon the intersecting differences of our anatomies and body politics at different points in time. Only hands, head, and feet touch the ground in this ongoing reconfiguration of boundaries between myself and (an)other. We emerge from a material process of *being* in relationship and exchanging movement phrasing over time. Every time I enter the *roda*, I move beyond the master narratives of biological determinism and social compliance by creating kinship through my repeated material-relational engagement.

Understanding intersubjectivity as a kinaesthetic and corporeal process highlights intra-activity—how we can dynamically shift between me and not me, and how we are both within and part of the world in our improvised becomings. This speaks to the developmental process that my witness identified:

> *I got really caught up in ... being able to assess you ... when you said you didn't know she [your mother] was unwell at that point or there was a sort of coming in and out of knowing...I couldn't make assessments around you as I was witnessing you, and I saw shape flow and smoothness and even tone and breath and ease and then I saw from your face it wasn't OK, it was like—ah, the confusion, the not being clear, not knowing. You weren't OK, and I could tell by your back and now you're saying kidneys, so—knowing-and-not-knowing, I got very caught up in that. And...I was panicked.*

During this unfolding movement exploration I understood how capoeira continues to assist my embodiment of the paradox of strength and fragility. My witness' use of the word "assess" is interesting here. For clinicians, assessment is an inevitable relational aspect of witnessing since it highlights the non-neutrality of seeing the other. This relationality has its roots in the early developmental process and research emphasizes the importance of the shared gaze and physical holding between adult and infant and how this shapes the child's development (Beebe, Knoblauch, Rustin, & Sorter, 2005). The mismatch between my movement and facial expression, which my witness picked up on, seems to resonate with the first vignette (*Birthday*) where I couldn't *see* my mother. Our gaze is no longer reciprocal—perhaps this evokes the *panic* that my witness experienced, and that I experienced, when I knew my mother was dying.

Writing-dancing this chapter has been a process of remembrance, a corporeal reclaiming after loss. In the re-storying of my embodied experiences I have been "transported" (Leahy et al., 2012) not only back in time but forward into a more nuanced embodied developmental understanding of my maternal lineage and my ability to access a material-discursive grounding in not-knowing. And yet, this transportation is paradoxical: my intra-actions with the materiality of movement and being witnessed creates new entangled understandings of, in Nancy Tuana's terms, a "viscous porosity" (2008) where politics, time, environments, bodies, and loss are thrown into sharp relief as inevitable aspects of our becomings in the existential process of loving-in-action.

NOTES

[1] Barad (2007) created the neologism of intra-action to denote the mutually constitutive process of being within and as part of the world rather than the more familiar use of inter-action of separate entities. She explains: "the notion of intra-action recognizes that distinct agencies do not precede, but rather emerge through, their intra-action" (p. 33).

[2] Gerry Harrison, colleague and friend with whom I have shared nearly two decades of kinship. Gerry began her career as a psychiatric nurse and, for the past two decades, has been practicing as a registered Dance Movement Psychotherapy clinician, supervisor and in private practice. Gerry has over thirty years experience of working in adult in-patient psychiatry within the NHS.

[3] Capoeira is an Afro-Brazilian art that combines dance and martial art.

[4] The berimbau is a single-stringed, musical bow with a hollow gourd resonator attached near the bottom.

[5] Translated as "master," as per martial practices that cultivate a relationship of master as mentor. Although I still find this naming problematic, the implicit hierarchy of this label is somewhat undermined in the often shortened and affectionate term "mest."

[6] Translated as "the game." In capoeira the jogo exists within a socio-cultural and historical system of African slavery and Portuguese colonization in Brazil.

[7] Translated as "fall on the kidneys," a capoeira position practiced close to the floor that involves folding the knees into the chest and balancing on either the left or right sides on the hands and elbows—the underside elbow presses into the kidney.

[8] The roda is the circle formed by *capoeiristas* (practitioners of capoeira) who sing and clap and are led by the *bateria* (orchestra). All proficient capoeiristas learn to play all of the musical instruments in the *bateria*.

REFERENCES

Alcoff, L. M. (2012). Gender and reproduction. In S. Gonzalez-Arnal, G. Jagger, & K. Lennon (eds.), *Embodied Selves* (pp. 12-28). New York: Palgrave Macmillan.

Allegranti, B. (Director). (2005). *In my body* [Film]. Cologne: Media Arts Productions.

Allegranti, B. (2011). *Embodied performances: Sexuality, gender, bodies.* New York: Palgrave Macmillan.

Allegranti, B. (2013). The politics of becoming bodies: Sex, gender and intersubjectivity in motion. *The Arts in Psychotherapy, 40*, 394-403.

Allegranti, B. (Director), & Wyatt, J. (Assistant Director). (2012). *Your story calls me* [Film]. London: Nest Films.

Allegranti, B., & Wyatt, J. (forthcoming). Witnessing loss: A feminist material discursive account. *Qualitative Inquiry.*

Allende, I. (1995). *Paula.* London: Harper Collins.

Barad, K. (2007). *Meeting the universe halfway: Quantum physics and the entanglement of matter and meaning.* Durham, NC: Duke University Press.

Beebe, B., Knoblauch, S., Rustin, S., & Sorter, D. (2005). *Forms of intersubjectivity in infant research and adult treatment.* New York: Other Press.

Butler, J. (1994). Against proper objects. *Differences: A Journal of Feminist Cultural Studies, 6*(2/3), 1-27.

Butler, J. (2006). *Precarious life: The powers of mourning and violence.* London: Verso.

Butler, J. (2010). *Frames of war: When is life grievable?* London: Verso.

Downey, G. (2005). *Learning capoeira: Lessons in cunning from an Afro-Brazilian art.* Oxford: Oxford University Press.

Fausto-Sterling, A. (2000). *Sexing the body: Gender politics and the construction of sexuality.* New York: Basic Books.

Finnegan, F. (2001). *Do penance or perish: Magdalene Asylums in Ireland.* Oxford: Oxford University Press.

Foucault, M. (1988). Technologies of the self. In L. Martin, H. Gutman, & P. Hutton (Eds.), *Technologies of the self: A seminar with Michel Foucault* (pp. 16-49). Amherst: University of Massachusetts Press.

Foucault, M. (1991). *Discipline and punish: The birth of the prison,* (A. Sheridan, Trans.). London: Penguin.

Gendlin, E. T. (1996). *Focusing-oriented psychotherapy: A manual of the experiential method.* New York: Guilford.

Grosz, E. (2005). *Time travels: Feminism. Nature. Power.* Durham, NC: Duke University Press.

Leahy, M. M., O'Dwyer, M. & Ryan, F. (2012). Witnessing stories: Definitional ceremonies in narrative therapy with adults who stutter. *Journal of Fluency Disorders, 37,* 234-241.

Marquez, G. G. (2007). *One hundred years of solitude.* London: Penguin.

Mindell, A. (1987). *The dreambody in relationships.* London: Penguin.

Oyama. S. (2000). *Evolution's eye: A systems view of the biology-culture divide.* Durham, NC: Duke University Press.

Sheets-Johnstone, M. (2000). Kinetic-tactile-kinesthetic bodies: Ontogenetical foundations of apprenticeship learning. *Human Studies, 23,* 343-370.

Trevarthen, C. (2004). Intimate contact from birth. In K. White (Ed.), *Touch: Attachment and the body* (pp. 1-16). London: Karnack Books.

Tuana, N. (2008). Viscous porosity: Witnessing Katrina. In S. Alaimo & S. Heckman (Eds.), *Material feminisms* (pp. 188-213). Bloomington: Indiana University Press.

White. M. (2000). *Reflections on narrative practice: Essays and interviews.* Adelaide: Dulwich Centre Publications.

Winnicott, D. (1971). *Playing and reality.* New York, NY: Routledge.

Young, I. (2005). *On female body experience: "Throwing Like a Girl" and other essays.* Oxford: Oxford University Press.

Drawings by Neil Max Emmanuel, for the author.

Beatrice Allegranti
Centre for Arts Therapies Research
University of Roehampton

67

ANNE M. HARRIS

GHOST-CHILD

A story is not just a story. Once the forces have been aroused and set into motion, they can't simply be stopped at someone's request. Once told, the story is bound to circulate; humanized it may have a temporary end, but its effects linger on and its end is never truly an end. (Trinh, 1989, p. 133)

FAMILY SNAPS #1: 6PM

Unseasonably cold in San Jose, I sit on her stoop while my girlfriend waits around the corner in a rental car. "Sitting on the stoop" here used as both truth/fiction, past/present. I am thirty years old and have travelled from New York, spurred on by a stranger's words that I am "daughter" to this "mother." I want to see her, just once.

She hides behind the curtains, behind a closed front door, and turns up the television.

"Go away!" she yells.

Her husband, Tony, mumbles, "Don't be like that, Dorothy."

Silence.

Light San Jose breeze.

Kids playing in the next street.

"Open the door," I say, flatly. "You might as well open the door."

"Go away," she says again, like a mantra, like a plea. "You're a ghost and I want you to leave."

*

For adoptees, both fantasy and fact play a role in our self-narratives, our performed biographies, our imaginaries of home. For those like me, visuality plays a role too in the search for family. I thought I needed to see my mother to believe in her; equally mistaken, she needed to not see me in order to maintain my erasure. This chapter is about absence as companion-mother, loss as ghost-daughter, and performing self at points of departure and returning.

Mother-daughter relationships are complicated at the best of times, and always ghost-like: for mothers, a daughter can be a shadow of what the mother once was; for daughters, the mother a foreshadow who never leaves us, not through death, absence, rejection or reproduction. She is always just there, at our elbow, on the breeze. Strangely, this is true even when we never knew her. This chapter is a performative autoethnography[1] about performing daughter to a hidden mother, a

J. Wyatt & T. E. Adams (eds.), On (Writing) Families, 69–75.

ghost-daughter to an unknown mother. How do you perform an identity you have never known?

HAUNTED HOME

My approach to my birthmother mirrors performative autoethnography, in that "the knowing body finds its power in the cognitive, affective, and intuitive coming together to form a sense of what it has to say" (Pelias, 2008, p. 187). Similarly, I didn't know what I would say to her when I mounted those steps, but I knew my body would guide me; performative inquiry at its best.

Trinh (1989) articulates the power of stories, particularly those within families and family cultures, by drawing direct and indirect lines between cultural diasporas and familial ones; between sex, gender and race displacement, and familial micro-communities, even imagined ones (Anderson, 2006). When we cannot perform our roles within known communities, or when those communities have outlived their usefulness, we imagine new ones. Performative autoethnography is one way in which I imagine new ones.

Visuality too is important in a process of performing the roles of daughter and mother, for both adoptee and queer diasporas (Eng, 2003; Patton & Sanchez-Eppler, 2000). We need to see the roles to believe them. Visuality embodies discourses in which self is established through repetitive intersubjective acts (Butler, 1990). But performing self sometimes has to occur in isolation, or ghost-like whispers, on stoops: a mono/autoethnography that refuses to be dialogic in the intersubjective world. Performance ethnographers (e.g., Holman Jones 2011; Langellier 2009; Pelias 2008; Spry, 2011) continue to help me make sense of the ways in which autoethnographing on a San Jose stoop for an afternoon in late spring could help me become the daughter who could let an unknown mother go.

My overriding fear about meeting my birthfamily—because I always knew I would find them—was linked to being gay. Do you have children? Are you married? I never imagined that she would not want to know anything. My struggle with making peace with being gay was not unrelated to my struggle to find and feel some belonging with my birthfamily. My feelings about the effects of my adoption and yearning to find family perfectly mirror Adams' (2011) description of coming out: "You struggle in your relationships. You don't want to be lonely but fear speaking….[you] dwell in confusion. You hate your abrasiveness with others but do not know how to act differently" (p. 68). Finding an unwilling birthmother is like confronting again the challenges of coming out: it's not the outing, but the way it triggers such deep desire to be accepted, that can be so crippling.

Patton and Sanchez-Eppler (2000) challenge the possibility of queer diasporic space as an imagined utopia in which "dislocated bodies may refind their native discourses when they get 'there'" (p. 10), as if "there" was a discernable destination. Pelias (borrowing from Dolan) argues how performance inquiry can help us stake "imaginative territories that map themselves over the real" (p. 192), much as I needed to map my own territory of daughterness over the refused landscape of motherness in San Jose. Queers, like adoptees, know that kinship often remains an imagined community (part fact, part fiction), yet deeply important to constructing a sense of belonging in the world, even when the world falls short (Harris, 2012; Harris & Gandolfo, 2013). My day on the stoop of my birthmother testified to my need for time, place and imagination in a performance of home.

Home as an embodiment—as my body—is at the heart of performance ethnographies. Kinship relationality (Langellier, 2009) can be reimagined by performative autoethnography because "narrative as embodied emphasizes the living presence of bodily contact" (Madison, 2005, p. 211), and this embodiment of mother-daughterness is what remains elusive for me, more than fifteen years after San Jose. The power of choosing a performative autoethnography to convey the subjective truth of that day is its ability to understand the other, even when the other is not there, unknowable, or hiding behind a curtain. "It is the dialogic relationship with the Other," Madison argues, "this ongoing liveliness and resistance to finality…that has adversely haunted traditional ethnography" (p. 10); this ability to confront haunted traditions (both ethnographic and personal) offers me a tool for re-approaching an ever-present Other who has been with me all of the time, but who refuses to open the door to intersubjectivity, enquiry, or recognition.

Being gay and adopted is pretty queer. Queering autoethnography and even adoption, however, is more than just writing one's self into the text. Queering autoethnography and adoption "asks questions about what *counts*—as experience, as knowledge, as scholarship, as opening up possibilities for doing things and being in the world differently" (Adams & Holman Jones, 2008, p. 376). Seeing others whom I resemble for the first time as a full-grown adult, and being told I'm a ghost, are two very queer experiences. Yet there are other, more subtle parallels: being gay still calls into question oneself in relation to others, as does being adopted. Family cannot be taken for granted. Nor can autoethnography, which is, as Adams and Holman Jones tell us, all about the "known and unknown, hidden and present, all at once" (p. 373).

FAMILY SNAPS #2: 10AM

Which truth? (Trinh, 1989, p. 120)

The scene that contextualises my opening goes something like this:

We pull up in front of a nondescript suburban San Jose house. The corner lot, two sides of her house face perpendicular streets. The stoop of her house faces us, and conjoined, the neighbour's stoop faces the other street.

My girlfriend tells me I have to do it alone, the same gauntlet she threw down when I met my grandmother in similar fashion, about six months prior. So while Vanessa sits in the car, I get out and nervously walk up the stoop, knock on the front door and wait. Knock again. Look around: a dog barks, a car drives by, slows to get a better look at me.

Nothing.

Vanessa points to the other house, semi-attached but miles away. I walk over, knock, and before my knuckles hit the door a second time, a middle-aged man yanks it open and stares through the screen door:

"Yeah?"

"I'm looking for the woman who lives next door—Dorothy?"

"Okay." Like I was asking for permission.

"Well, there's no answer, and um ... being Sunday ... Do you think they're at church or something?"

"I don't know."

"Know when they'll be back?"

"Nah," he says. "Should I tell her who dropped by?"

And without wasting a beat, I make stalker mistake #1: I tell him the truth.

"Yeah, I'm her daughter." It caught in my throat a bit but its smoothness was a victory.

"Okay." And he shuts the door.

I didn't think it through. I wasn't used to subterfuge (her word, not mine).

I go back to the car where Vanessa's reading.

"Nothing?"

"No," I say. "Let's come back later."

We'd driven all the way up from her dad's in Los Angeles (LA), on the spur of the moment before our flight back to New York the next day—because I had a gut feeling that it would be a great meeting.

"Where are we supposed to go? We don't know anyone in San Jose!" she says. "Maybe we should just sit here and wait."

"That guy'll probably call the cops," I say. "He was kinda creepy."

"You didn't tell him who you are, did you?" she says, and before she finishes the sentence, I'm crying.

"That was dumb," she says. "We might as well go then. Dorothy will avoid this house for a week if she knows you're looking for her."

"How was I supposed to know?!"

We drive around the neighbourhood and try (unsuccessfully) to imagine her life. We go to McDonalds and sit there refusing to eat anything.

An hour later we return. This time, Vanessa tells me to park around the side, so I do. We sit there for a while.

"Are you gonna do it? Cuz if you're not gonna do it let's just leave. I'm starving and we have to drive all the way back to LA."

I do it. I get out and head toward the front corner of the house, Vanessa jumping out behind me and getting in the driver's seat.

"I'll keep the car running in case we need to make a quick getaway!"

I walk up the stoop again and, this time, I hear television sounds, and a man and woman's voices talking indistinctly to one another.

I walk up and ring the bell, hopeful.

"Who is it?" she says and my heart lurches.

My bad feeling is growing.

"Census!" I say.

Nothing.

"Census, please. I need to check a few details."

Nothing.

"Ma'am? Could you open the door please?"

(Pause.)

"I know who you are," she says. "I know who you are and I want you to leave. I'm not going to open the door."

Muffled arguing. The television gets louder.

"I'm not leaving!" I shout. I see the man from this morning behind his screen.

There is a ruffling of curtains near her door, and I see a plump face with round glasses.

"That's cheating!" I yell. "If I can't see you, you can't see me!" and I turn my back to her but refuse to leave.

The standoff continues.

"I'll call the cops!" she yells.

"Do it. What are you gonna tell them, your daughter is on your stoop? That'll be a good show for your creepy neighbour."

(Pause.)

She keeps shifting from one window to the next, peeping out until I look up, then pulling away. What a tease.

"You're a ghost and I want you to leave."

"I'm not a ghost," I say, but she doesn't hear me. No one hears me.

"I'm not a ghost, I'm a person," I say again.

Nothing.

I sit down.

For a while I cry. Then I sob. I sit there for more than five hours, and she never opens the door.

*

I speak everything I ever needed to say, everything I've dreamed of saying for so many years. It doesn't matter in the end that no one heard me. All of a sudden, something shifts, the pain eases.

It comes like a sentence:

"There's nothing here for me."

It's my release. I realise she can't give me anything I crave, that the mother I dreamed of is gone. What's done is done. Dorothy is a ghost too.

I see myself from a distance, over the thirty years leading up to that day, and it seems to me in that moment that I have spent my entire life banging on somebody's metaphorical door wanting to be let in.

I suddenly feel free.

I stand up, wipe my eyes, and walk away.

When I round the corner onto the side street, Vanessa jumps out of the car (now turned off, thankfully) and rushes to embrace me.

"Are you ok?"

"I didn't meet her," I say.

"I know," she says. "I was watching. What a bitch."

"It took a while, but I think I'm free. Let's go home."

ANNE M. HARRIS

NAMING OUR SELVES

There is a price for telling the truth about yourself and for the loss—or disavowal—of such knowledge. (Holman Jones, 2011, p. 333)

Trinh (1989) reminds us of the narrative truth that "when we insist on telling over and over again, we insist on repetition in re-creation (and vice versa) .... Each story is at once a fragment and a whole; a whole within a whole" (p. 123). My stories have kept me alive in a sense, but it is equally true that my stories (in place of Story) have cost me something. Like more traditional ethnographers, I go out into the field of my life, and work myself like an Other, in relation to others, using story undistinguished between fact/fiction to "inform the explanations [I] invented for the things [I] did not understand" (Cather, cited in Trinh, 1989, p. 124). By using the empathic body in performative autoethnographies, we can ask the "'magic if': If I were in that situation, what would I do and feel?" (Pelias, 2008, p. 187) in deeper ways than even the lived moment may allow. In performative autoethnography, I can ask myself the question that the embodied moment of (non)meeting my birthmother foreclosed: *how does she feel?* It was a pivotal day for me, obviously. I felt liberated for a long time after that, and I retold this story countless times, joyfully. I met the rest of my birthfamily, and I healed in some ways. Part of that healing was to believe that I had finally—in that symbolic act of sitting on her stoop for so long without relief—liberated myself from the bondage of wanting to belong, always begging to be let into other peoples' lives, hearts, spaces.

It worked for a while. But what I realised as time went by was that loss and absence are not so easily resolved—they take on a life of their own. Like woodturning on a lathe, life provides the ever-returning opportunity to cut a bit more away and shape the vessel more intricately, to smooth out the surfaces, to perfect the rough emotion of loss. But it is never finished, never still, just a constant turning and returning. As time went on, the language of recovery or healing sounded more and more absurd, more like a lie than it did that first victorious day off the stoop. I would hear myself telling the story to people who invariably stood aghast at the pain of the story, only to have me reassure them insipidly, "No, it's all good, I feel liberated and whole. I've come to appreciate myself and my circumstance," and so on. Whatever bullshit story I could neatly wrap it up in always came up short.

Langellier asks the question that so many queer and adoptee diasporic travellers ask ourselves ceaselessly: "How do we 'name our own' as performance?" (2009, p. 127) Performance, she insists, is "in dialogue with absent or 'ghostly audiences'" (p. 127). That has certainly been true for me. Performative autoethnography gives me a chance to be in dialogue with those who are gone, those who have never appeared, and those who are there but not visible, not audible, silent. In this way, life is perhaps the most radical performative autoethnography imaginable.

NOTES

[1] Here I take Spry's (2011) use of performative autoethnography, one in which "For a performative autoethnographer, the critical stance of the performing body constitutes a praxis of evidence and analysis. We offer our performing body as raw data of a critical cultural story" (p. 19).

REFERENCES

Adams, T. E. (2011). *Narrating the closet: An autoethnography of same-sex attraction.* Walnut Creek, CA: Left Coast Press.

Adams, T. E., & Holman Jones, S. (2008). Autoethnography is queer. In N. K. Denzin, Y. S. Lincoln, & L. T. Smith (Eds.), *Handbook of critical and indigenous methodologies* (pp. 373-390). Thousand Oaks, CA: Sage.

Anderson, B. (2006). *Imagined communities: Reflections on the origin and spread of nationalism.* London: Verso.

Butler, J. (1990). *Gender trouble.* New York: Routledge.

Eng, D. L. (2003). Transnational adoption and queer diasporas. *Social Text, 76,* 1-37.

Harris, A., & Gandolfo, E. (2013). Looked at and looked over or: I wish I was adopted. *Gender, Place & Culture: A Journal of Feminist Geography.*

Harris, A. (2012). Queer refugeities and the problematics of homo/homelands. *Gay and Lesbian Issues and Psychology Review, 8,* 22-33.

Holman Jones, S. (2011). Lost and found. *Text and performance Quarterly, 31,* 322-341.

Langellier, K. M. (2009). Personal narrative, performance, performativity: Two or three things I know for sure. *Text and Performance Quarterly, 19,* 125-144.

Madison, D. S. (2005). *Critical ethnography: Method, ethics, and performance.* Thousand Oaks, CA: Sage.

Patton, C., & Sanchez-Eppler, B. (Eds.). (2000). *Queer diasporas.* Durham, NC: Duke University Press.

Pelias, R. (2008). Performative inquiry: Embodiment and its challenges. In J. G. Knowles & A. L. Cole (Eds.), *Handbook of the arts in qualitative research* (pp. 185-194). Thousand Oaks: Sage.

Spry, T. (2011). *Body, paper, stage: Writing and performing autoethnography.* Walnut Creek, CA: Left Coast Press.

Trinh, T. M. (1989). *Woman, native, other: Writing postcoloniality and feminism.* Bloomington, IN: Indiana University Press.

Anne Harris
Faculty of Education
Monash University

JEANNIE WRIGHT

LIVING PLACES[1]

"The biography of a person is intimately bound up with objects."
—Sarah Ahmed, *The Promise of Happiness*

I just set the fire alarm off. The rented flat (last of several in the last two years of living as an academic migrant) has an efficient and very loud fire alarm. I'm writing, eating, and didn't notice the smell and the smoke.

The noise panics me. I don't know the cooker well enough to turn it off fully and plantains have burned badly in the frying pan. I throw windows open, waft tea towels over the sensor. There's a grey box in the hallway where the noise is coming from. Never knew what it was for. Turn the key and a flap opens. There's a button that says, "Reset alarm." I press it and the noise stops. Breathe out. Throw more windows open.

On the same grey box in the hallway, so that it's the first thing I see when I come in the door, I stuck a card. My daughter sent it to me on Mother's Day. It shows a blond, blue-eyed, curly-haired little girl, who is maybe 5 years old. It says: "*Mommy, when I grow up I want to help smash the white racist, homophobia, patriarchy, bull-shit paradigms too!*"

I love this card. It's not the kind of card I send my mum, and it serves the same purpose. We are marking how lucky it is, to be a mother/daughter—mocking traditional, commercial Mother's Day cards—and just taking the opportunity to have a laugh. Share a laugh.

You would never cook plantains, mum. Your good cooking was plain and English. Meat and potato pie, starting from scratch with peeling vegetables and rolling out the pastry with an empty milk bottle.

Dear mum
I sent you a card on Mother's Day.
Not that you could read it.
It rhymed.
I miss laughing with you.
Your laugh, fierce, irreverent.
Hips broken and reset.
Dancing with walking frames.
No cure for old age, eh,
I'm sorry mum.

J. Wyatt & T. E. Adams (eds.), On (Writing) Families, 77–83.

I wish I could have flown you away,
Danced you away,
Sung you away and not left you in that hospital.
If you had been born in a different age, and richer, you might have been
suffragette, a feminista.

Dear aunties, mothers, cousins
You work as cleaners.
I've seen you cleaning
steps at the University where I teach.
You also do evening shifts in factories,
near where you live so that you can walk
there and back.
You'd come home smelling
of what you'd been working with,
tobacco from the Player's factory (now closed),
talc and bath cubes from the Cusson's factory (now closed).

AUTOETHNOGRAPHY AND ETHICS

There will be no photographs of my family in this writing. Consent is difficult
enough even when people are alive. I warn the students, who decide they want to
write autoethnographic narratives,
    "It's not an easy option. Especially the ethical issues. Read Chang (2008)."
    And some of them do.
    "Chang (2008) is particularly strong on ethics," I say.
    These are counseling and psychotherapy students, and Jane Speedy's (2008,
2013) writing makes the most sense to them, yet they don't get it, the exposure,
until they've started writing.
    I remember a presenter at a gender and education conference in the late 1990s.
She started to talk about personal disclosure in autoethnographic narratives and the
level of exposure. She said, "This far and no further," and she started to take off
her cardigan, then her shirt, then her T-shirt. It seemed as if everybody in the room
stopped breathing. Underneath her last layer was a swimming costume—prim and
high-necked. Loud laughter and relief? We didn't even get a glimpse of her
underwear—did we want to? (Ellis, Bochner, Denzin, Goodall, Pelias, &
Richardson, 2007).

POETIC INQUIRY

As well as working out where the bridges between social classes lead away from
and towards, this chapter is about the loss of my parents, about them and their
social class and me and my feminisms, and about our relationship. One aim in this
writing is self-healing (Foucault, 1997). Though critical of theories of the "inner-
self," I'm conscious of competing psychological theories in the context of loss, and

skeptical about all of them. One of the tensions my parents' deaths has tightened is the divide between parents of one social class and their children who are educated out of those origins (Ballinger & Wright, 2007). "They" would never have gone near a therapist. I've tried therapy and found self-writing more effective, less stigmatizing and cheaper. Writing brings relief.

I want to avoid sentimentality and labeling about grief, and about the class I was born into. Laurel Richardson nails it, "I am afraid of the crowd, but I don't label it *crowd*, I label the people *working class*. I am afraid of the working class" (Richardson, 2005, p. 486). It would be relatively easy to locate this writing explicitly by taking photographs of the state housing we used to live in, of "them" at work and at home. Instead I will take photographs of a cookbook. It represents some of the cultural envelope within which this narrative fits, the nexus of self and culture (Pelias, 2004). Whether (im)possible or not, I'm also writing the self with a feminist view, the personal and the political interacting (Gannon, 2006).

This is writing from the heart and poetic inquiry attempts to carry some of the sensory, emotional, embodied ambiguities of experience. *Walking My Mother*, Butler-Kisber's (2010) poem, does just that (p. 96).

COOKBOOKS

In 2006, 10 years after my dad died, I migrated to Aotearoa, New Zealand. The packers filled crates and the crates stayed in the container and the container stayed on the deck, all the way through the shipping lanes. Three months later the boxes arrived. The two cookbooks I'd inherited were there, in the boxes and eventually got unpacked. They sat on the shelves in my new kitchen on the other side of the planet. I thought I was going for good, maybe—but those two books were some of the few to come back with me to the UK five years later. More containers, packers …. One reason to migrate is to avoid the unrelenting British class system.

A friend from Liverpool, of similar age and class background, picked the cookbooks up in my New Zealand kitchen and said, "Oh, taonga!" (A Maori word that could roughly be translated as "treasure" or "heritage.")

We laughed.

One of the things I learned in New Zealand is the reverence for "taonga," for treasure associated with family and with place. These books are treasures, connecting me to the street in inner city Nottingham, the row of houses, the front room, blue air and nicotine-stained ceiling, and my dad smoking his twentieth, maybe thirtieth, Park Drive tipped of the day. We saved the coupons, and saved up for a cookbook.

Cooking With Men in Mind is a small paperback specially produced for the tobacco company, Gallaher Ltd., sometime in the 1960s, by Queen Anne Press (London). There is no date on the inside cover. The introduction, by Betty Hitchcock, starts with, "There is no doubt about it, the subtle way to a man's heart is by way of his stomach, though you may well pass off your efforts as a mere interest in his health and well-being" (p. 5).

How many hundreds of cigarettes did my dad smoke to trade for this book? He started smoking when he left school at 14. He died of a heart attack in 1996, at the age of 76.

The book is creased, pages yellowed, worn away on the cover. Betty   Hitchcock continues,

> Keeping the "inner man" well fed is not difficult. Many a man longs for some good old-fashioned home cooking. Luncheon voucher meals, business lunches, or dinners, though serving their purpose, bear no comparison to the meals a man's mother used to make! (p. 5)

On the inside cover at some point in the 1960s, I have stapled a cutout from *Budget Bites*, the local newspaper. I wanted to be able to produce pastry like my mother. I didn't want to be the smiling woman in the apron standing behind the man on the cover of the book. Around this time, in my mid-teens, I stopped eating meat. Most of the recipes feature meat, budget cuts: corned beef, luncheon meat, liver and onions, chicken wings, sausage, bacon, oxtail stew. Why did we need this book? My mother learned from her mother; she had no need for a cookbook.

FEMINISTA

The contradictions: I want to cook and know how to feed people well, like my mother does. I don't want to be a girl. I'm the third daughter, the one who definitely should have been a boy. I follow dad around, help him with shoveling horse manure for the back yard when the brewery wagon delivers to the pub at the back of the house. Tall, I have short hair, wear trousers.

As I get older, I'm a killjoy. When other people's happiness means following a white, heteronormative, patriarchal orientation, you have to kill their joy as a political act (Ahmed, 2010). What was left? When I started University and joined the Women's Group, not much.

1971, in the kitchen. My dad's smoking—probably Park Drive tipped.

"What did I ever do to you?"

His tone is angry. This question accuses and underneath somewhere he's hurt. It is an accusation and an appeal. When I look at his eyes, the same grey as mine, I can see he's confused.

"Nothing!" I say, and it's true. He's a good dad.

Of course when I rant about patriarchy or leave some of the feminist leaflets I hand out at university and outside factories lying around the house, it's not my dad I'm talking about. He's a very gentle man. OK, he doesn't cook and doesn't wash, neither does my brother, and I do point this out mostly at meal times. There's not a lot of space to argue. Two rooms downstairs.

In dreams I still see dad. He's usually on my side.

Dear dad
I'm still very sorry I couldn't cut your toenails.
I'm just not that sort of daughter.

WHY I'M A COUNSELOR, NOT A CHIROPODIST

When my dad was dying,
That April,
He couldn't bend to cut his toenails.
He sat there, heaving for breath,
I sat there, making
Excuses:
The chiropodist will come.
What about the nurses?
I didn't know he was dying.
And when he had,
All through May I woke up sweating
Seeing him, sitting up in the ward
With the oxygen mask over his mouth
Worrying about asking someone
A stranger
To cut his toenails.

He didn't know he was dying.
I could listen as he talked,
Mostly about the War and pre-War,
Stories of scams and slow foxtrots.
When it was time for the mask again,
Stopping words,
I'd bent over and kissed him.
Walking out of the ward, bright with tulips,
I did look back and see him
Sitting up in bed, breathing. (Wright, 2003)

REFERENCE POINTS

One friend emailed after mum died and said, "That's another lost reference point."

It grates, harsh and official, and I don't respond.

It is though, she's right, another lost reference point. The Park Drive *Cooking With Men in Mind*—who do I know who would "get" these references?

My daughter, Katie, who is currently more immersed in academic texts than me, pointed out Sara Ahmed's use of "killjoy feminist" and emails me an analysis of this chapter: "*Cooking With Men in Mind* was an object grandma kept in proximity as a promise of happiness as a good wife, mother—you keep it near out of nostalgia, charged with emotion as a problematic/ironic/loving object connecting you with your mum but, at the same time, distancing you, reminding you about your political differences. Conflicting desires to be a good cook, good mum but to reject patriarchy as oppressive."

"We never listened to anything so lowbrow," a friend says, when I'm joking about sneaking into the kitchen and re-tuning the radio away from dad's choice of music. I don't respond and think about what "lowbrow" means. We are lowbrow, we rent the house from the council, we live in a part of the city that's becoming full of migrants from India and the West Indies. Way before ethnic anything becomes fashionable. As the artist Grayson Perry would say, "it's all a question of taste."

GRIEVING

The comfort of trees and being outside is most real and dependable at this time. Too much winter. Wherever you are mum, I hope it's warm and there's dancing every day.

Meanwhile the wild geese, high in the clean blue air,
are heading home again.
Whoever you are, no matter how lonely,
the world offers itself to your imagination,
calls to you like the wild geese, harsh and exciting–
over and over announcing your place
in the family of things. (Oliver, 1992)

Where I fit in the family of things is less certain now, less warm than when I used to watch old black and white films on Saturday afternoons in the front room with mum. She was reliable. I don't find many people reliable at this time.

Mary Oliver's poem, *Wild Geese*, is taped to my bathroom wall. Since mum died in March I've been memorising it. It's soothing to recite it, silently, when I'm brushing my teeth. Don't know about this last stanza though.

On a grey day I'm sitting near the artificial lake at work, around this time of numbness and dizziness. I can't seem to connect with the ground. I like the lake and the trees and tend to avoid the mess the geese leave behind.

The wild geese are in a panic; they're in disarray. A great flapping of wings against the water and they take off, flying low towards me in a gang, honking.

NOTES

[1] I acknowledge Katie Wright Higgins's analysis.

REFERENCES

Ahmed, S. (2010). *The promise of happiness*. Durham, NC: Duke University Press.

Ballinger, E., & Wright, J. K. (2007). Does class count? Social class and counselling. *Counselling and Psychotherapy Research, 7*, 157-163.

Butler-Kisber, L. (2010). *Qualitative inquiry: Thematic, narrative and arts-informed perspectives*. London: Sage.

Chang, H. (2008). *Autoethnography as method*. Walnut Creek, CA: Left Coast Press.

Ellis, C., Bochner, A. P., Denzin, N. K., Goodall, H. L., Pelias, R., & Richardson, L. (2007). Coda: Let's get personal. In N. K. Denzin & M. D. Giardina (Eds.), *Ethical futures in qualitative research: Decolonizing the politics of knowledge* (pp. 220-267). Walnut Creek, CA: Left Coast Press.

Foucault, M. (1997). Technologies of the self. In P. Rabinow (Ed.), *Ethics: Subjectivity and truth. Essential works of Foucault 1954-1984* (pp. 223-252). London: Penguin.

Gannon, S. (2006). The (im)possibilities of writing the self-writing: French poststructural theory and autoethnography. *Cultural Studies↔Critical Methodologies, 6*, 474-495.

Oliver, M. (1992). *New and selected poems*. Boston: Beacon Press.

Pelias, R. J. (2004). *A methodology of the heart: Evoking academic and daily life*. Walnut Creek, CA: AltaMira Press.

Richardson, L. (2005). Sticks and stones: An exploration of the embodiment of social classism. *Qualitative Inquiry, 11*, 485-491.

Speedy, J. (2008). *Narrative inquiry and psychotherapy*. Basingstoke: Palgrave Macmillan.

Speedy, J. (2013). Where the wild dreams are: Fragments from the spaces between research, writing, autoethnography, and psychotherapy. *Quantitative Inquiry, 19*, 27-34.

Wright, J. K. (2003). Writing for protection: Reflective practice as a counsellor. *Journal of Poetry Therapy, 16*, 191-198.

Jeannie Wright
Centre for Lifelong Learning
University of Warwick

ROBIN M. BOYLORN

MY DADDY IS SLICK, BROWN, AND COOL LIKE ICE WATER

PRELUDE: ON FATHERS AND LOVERS

Referencing whitewashed popular culture examples of "good" fathers, bell hooks (2004) refers to Cliff Huxtable[1] as a fantasy:

> Lovable, kind, a protector, and a provider, our fantasy black dad was funny; he had the ability to eliminate pain by making us laugh. There was never any rage or abuse or emotional neglect of any kind on *The Cosby Show*. (p. 102)

Cliff Huxtable was the daddy of my dreams, a black Prince Charming who was intentional about parenting. He was smart, handsome, caring and affectionate. His everyday presence in the lives of his children, alongside class privilege, made him the kind of father black folk could be proud of and black children wished for. hooks, however, challenges the assumption that black fathers being present in the home would be a panacea for black family life because they would not offer protection against patriarchy. She argues that the father-hunger of children in homes where fathers are present but abusive can be as intense as the father-absence felt by children in fatherless homes.

In this chapter, I chronicle my obsessive relationship with my father, through his absence, in my childhood and adulthood. I poetically compare my deep desire to be a daddy's girl with the reality of fatherlessness for significant portions of my life. I contemplate and negotiate the love/hate relationship I have with my father and how I transfer my experiences with my father to other black men. I link my relationship with my father to my relationship to potential romantic partners who are also black men as a way of engaging, theorizing, and seeking to understand how and why my father's absence has had a profound influence on my ability to have meaningful relationships with other men.

The layers of narrative represent the complicated nature of both my relationship with my father and my relationship with would-be romantic partners who, like my father, offer me conditional and arms-length love. The excerpts are in conversation with one another as interconnected moments, memories and responses to loss, rejection, and disappointment. At times, I am referencing, in reflection, my feelings in response to my father's rejection, while at other times I refer to experiences with other black men. The blending of those moments are intentional and significant because I attribute my father's absence with my failed attempts at romantic relationships. I blend my feelings and reflections on my father and black men I have encountered intimately to figure out how and why parallels exist between

J. Wyatt & T. E. Adams (eds.), On (Writing) Families, 85–93.

those relationships. I also attempt to reflect on my father's potential motives because I want to understand how someone can be absent in the life of someone he cares deeply about. I wonder if my father being more present in my life would have made a positive or significant difference. Finally, I consider my own accountability and responsibility for rectifying my relationship with my father.

I

My daddy is slick, brown, and cool like ice water in the desert. Charm makes up for his flaws, which are adequately covered by a handsome face and calm demeanor. When I was little he would wear layers of fashionable clothes that made him look like he was always either leaving or going someplace important. His style was flawless and I was proud to be his only biological child. At the time, I was the only thing in the world just like him. His brief stint in the military left him suave and sophisticated, so he knew how to stand like a soldier, roll a joint, talk shit, and take names. He wasn't ancient and serious like the black men I grew used to in the country. He was something else, my daddy, soulful, sentimental and believable. I could see why my mama, and every other grown woman with a mind to be noticed, was taken by him. I was taken by him. He was a sweet-talker with a honey-dipped tongue that would make you believe any lie he could tell. His sepia-shade sprung forth from his light-skinned, heavy-tongued mother whom I never knew, and his pecan skinned and slanted-eyed father who I can't remember. The color of Hennessy with remarkably dark eyes and a close cut beard, my daddy was unmistakably masculine and fiiiiiiiiiiine. In the 1980s he was everything. His intermittent presence was a combination of Christmas Eve anticipation and heartbreak. I missed him desperately. I loved him fiercely. The lonely days of my childhood were punctuated by his every-now-and-then visits.

II

I was color struck. When I was growing up, I had a crush on anything yellow-skinned and pretty eyed. My preference for pretty boys was linked to how they put me in the mind of my daddy. Not in the way they looked (my daddy was brown, not yellow) but in the way they carried themselves with their chin up, shoulders back, and quirky smirk on their faces walking around in the world poor and black like me, but feeling important and entitled. I wanted some of that confidence and cool to rub off on me. I felt that if a beautiful boy chose me it would make up for not being chosen by my father.

III

My daddy is not mean and harsh like other daddies. He never raises his voice or his hand at me. My mama does the heavy-lifting, the heavy-parenting because she is there all the time. Daddy has the luxury of getting me on my best behavior. He doesn't enforce rules or dictate bedtimes because he doesn't have to deal with the consequences. He is never there to wake me up in the morning. He doesn't have to live with a ten-year old temperament. He thinks my sassiness is cute, while my mama regularly threatens me over it.

IV

I can't stand him. He makes me feel like I am not (good) enough. Sometimes, the thought of him makes me sick. I resent how he would leave for days and weeks, and then show up smelling good and looking good and waiting for affection. I was an afterthought, the person he thought about after he had already passed out his time to everyone else, yet he expects me to love him, even though he hasn't done anything to earn my love. And God help me, I do love him. I can't help it. Even though his perpetual absence makes me feel self-conscious, I can't imagine my life without him. I have been in love with him for as long as I can remember. Loving him is like a bad habit I can't break. I crave his attention like a cigarette after sex, or something sweet after dinner.

V

Mama doesn't talk to me about my daddy, except to tell me what I do, just like him, that gets on her damn nerves. Or to threaten to tell him about my bad behavior. Or to tell me to get ready because he is picking my sister and me up for a visit. Or to remind me that it is his birthday.

Mama doesn't talk about my daddy or her daddy, except to tell me that her daddy left when she was around my age.

Mama doesn't talk about love, sex, or relationships, except to tell me to be careful.

VI

My daddy is a ladies' man. A rolling stone. But he can't help it. There is too much living for a beautiful black man to do, too much loving, too much jiving, too much scheming, too many distractions to be tied down by fatherhood. He didn't know what being a daddy would be like. He jumped in, head first, marrying my mama while she was pregnant with somebody else's baby. He wanted a baby that would belong to him and look like him, so he convinced my mama to make another baby out of desperation and love. Two girls two years apart and he was only two decades in his life. What did we expect him to do? Give up the high life for a slow life? I imagine the babygirl screams made him antsy. When his mama died, while I was still an arm baby, he sought comfort from women who looked like his mama. And my mama didn't look like her.

ROBIN M. BOYLORN

VII

He loves me.

On our first date, he bought me a meal at a French restaurant so fancy I couldn't read the menu. And he held my hand while he walked me home. The kiss tasted like rain, Tequila and Thursday. The kiss didn't say goodbye, it said stay the night, so he did. We made love until Friday, with me pretending that making love was the same as love.

He loves me not.

He promised to call me later. He didn't.

He loves me.

When my birthday was ten days away he seems interested and asks for my address. I smile the numbers and words giving him the information I imagine him writing down to send me a gift. I am flattered, humbled, excited.

He loves me not.

My birthday comes and goes and he doesn't remember. He doesn't call. He doesn't send a gift. It doesn't matter. I don't matter. He can't see me past his own needs.

I have never received a birthday gift from a man.

VIII

He was the first of many men to leave me for a light skinned woman. He was probably oblivious to the obviousness of it all. Light skin meant pretty and a trophy to wear on your arm. I was too brown, nappy-haired, thick lipped, just like him, nothing extraordinary. He had to find something to look at that didn't look like him, that didn't look like need.

For years I would cry into tear-soaked pillows praying, begging to wake up different. Maybe if I weren't so black my daddy would love me. Maybe if I were caramel-coated men would pick me.

IX

New Years,
Valentine's Day,
my birthday and Christmas
passed with no gift or regard,
but the grocery-store-bought
dozen red roses
with the apology card
meant he was sorry
for lying,
being emotionally and verbally abusive,
and having a girlfriend and another baby.
He expected rotting ass flowers to fix what he had broken.

X

My sister's daddy was not my daddy but we shared mine. Her father was a more permanent absent, showing up fewer times than I can count on one hand with gifts for her and no apology. When I asked who the handsome stranger was with my sister's eyes and lips I was told it was "her" daddy. I resented, for a while, that she got to have two daddies. Hers was hers, and mine was ours. But I would often forget she had a different and extra father because his visits were so inconsistent. It was normal for fathers to only come around when they felt like it. But they always came with gifts. Our daddy never came empty-handed.

XI

Somehow I always end up being the other woman. Could this be some daddy-issues-type-shit, or am I just the most naïve woman ever? In her book, *Whatever Happened to Daddy's Little Girl? The Impact of Fatherlessness on Black Women*, Jonetta Barras writes, "A girl abandoned by the first man in her life forever entertains powerful feelings of being unworthy or incapable of receiving any man's love" (p. 1).

I have seen the same patterns of inconsistency in my so-called romantic relationships. I unconsciously attract men just like my father: Pretty-boy-womanizers with no intention of settling down.

XII

My daddy didn't have time to slow down to watch me grow. He couldn't be there for the everydayness of my childhood but he showed up in increments, when his lifestyle and girlfriend permitted, bringing me twenty dollar bills and penny candy like they would make up for lost time.

The daddies in my family, my uncles and the husbands of cousins, were just like my daddy. They lived in different houses or slept all day and worked all night. They did not spend time with children—that was women's work. Daddies were for discipline and birthday parties. Daddies came around to see baby mamas, not their children.

I didn't realize daddies lived in the same house with their children until I was in the third grade and visited a friend's house. Her daddy was there, doing daddy-daughter things with her. He did the things my daddy did when he came around, but he did them all the time. I didn't understand why I didn't have a live-in daddy, an everyday, not-just-special-occasion daddy.

XIII

We never go to daddy's house because he lives with another woman. He also lives more than an hour away. I convince myself that he can't come more often because it takes too long. It's not his fault. When he promises that he will come, I wait on the steps, counting cars when they pass. I soon figure something important must have come up or he would call. When he doesn't call and mama finally makes me go in the house because it is getting dark outside and bugs are biting, I don't blame him—I blame her, I blame myself. I suspect that she told him to stay away. I think that perhaps I have done something to offend him. I promise, in prayer, that I won't be so worrisome next time I see him. I stop counting the times he doesn't come when he is supposed to. I stop inviting him to school functions. I stop expecting him to show up.

XIV

When my father visited he took up all of the oxygen in the room. Everyone rushed to cater to his needs. Fix him a plate, move over to make a place for him to sit, see what city smells and words he would pour out to impress us. He didn't talk much and when he did his voice was so deep you had to concentrate on his words in order to decipher them. He wore a ring on the fourth finger of his right hand, but it wasn't a wedding ring. His marriage to my mother was like a secret no one ever talked about. They were separated and lived separate lives. They dealt with each other like old friends who happened to have children together, only occasionally and surreptitiously touching each other like former lovers.

XV

I was so desperate for love, attention and affection from a man that I let the first boy who called me pretty put his hands between my legs. No one had ever told me I was pretty before. My daddy saved his sweet talk for grown women.

XVI

Our adult child-parent conversations are often about my so-called inadequacies. He challenges my life choices, doesn't understand why I don't "have a man" or why I am not desperate to "have children." He focuses on what he views as my failures instead of acknowledging my career and academic success. I feel that judgment echoed in the eyes of men I am interested in. They are only willing to offer me temporary and borrowed time, and any compliments come early but not often. They seem intimidated by my accomplishments, seeing them as reasons to reject me.

XVII

I get mad every time somebody says I look like my daddy. Part of my annoyance is that I don't feel like I know enough about him, or have ever concentrated on his face long enough, to recognize any resemblance. He never tells me I look like him. He has never told me I was pretty.

XVIII

Father's Day is always a dilemma because I can't find a card that represents my relationship with my father. They don't have deadbeat daddy cards. Hallmark promotes the father who is present and proud, usually white, and traditional. My daddy was preoccupied when I was growing up and even though I don't doubt that he loved me, he was too selfish to take care of me in any way that mattered. I grew up in a fatherless family dreaming about fictional fathers on tv. I wanted Cliff Huxtable to be my daddy. He was the daddy of my dreams, the epitome of provider, protector, hero. It didn't occur to me that Cliff Huxtable was the figment of someone's imagination, and not necessarily a real-life depiction of a black father. The only thing that mattered was that he was a father of four daughters whom he actively adored. He hugged and kissed his children. He teased and laughed with them. He looked over homework and inspected report cards. He was a disciplinarian. He inspected and intimated the boys who liked his daughters. He was loving, compassionate, funny, spirited and authentic. Sometimes I pretended Cliff Huxtable was my daddy.

INTERLUDE: FATHER FANTASIES

Perhaps my hegemonic fantasies about my daddy being present were unfair given the circumstances of our lives. Maybe he really didn't know any better. I don't think he intentionally hurt me, and I suspect there are structural reasons for his failure at fatherhood. He tried. He is not lacking from every memory of my childhood. His presence pushes memories to the forefront because his presence was such an extraordinary occurrence, a delicious experience. I remember riding bikes, eating ice cream, going to the park, play-swimming in the pool, Pizza Hut lunches, cab rides and Christmas mornings. Being with him was an adventure. And even though he was unable to live up to my expectations, I wonder whose fault that is—they're my expectations, not his.

There are social and cultural issues linked to racism and classism that affect black men in significant and unique ways. Perhaps my father's inability to live up to an ideal representation of fatherhood is rooted in his black manhood. Maybe the constraints, oppressions, and social issues affiliated with being a black man motivated him to be ill-equipped to be a father for the same reason the black men I have encountered romantically are unprepared to participate in a functional intimate relationship. As much as I grapple with my pain of fatherlessness, I also want to acknowledge the possibility of my father's pain because he failed at fathering me. As a black woman I can talk about my pain as long as it is tempered with strength and anger to substitute vulnerability (see Boylorn, 2014). However, my father, as a black man, must shield his pain under a mask of invulnerability (Majors & Billson, 1992).

I am not interested in letting my father off the hook entirely for his absence in my life, but I am also not invested in demonizing him. He is not a bad person—he was just not a good father. There is a difference. Maybe he didn't know how to be a good father. Maybe there was no one, including his own father, to teach him what being a good father meant. Maybe his performance of black masculinity jeopardized his ability to prioritize his child's needs over his own. Maybe the reasons for father absence in the black community are structural rather than intentional. Unfortunately, the emotional consequences are consistent regardless of the circumstances.

XIX

We had an adult heart-to-heart conversation over cafeteria food before I moved from North Carolina to Florida. I agreed, reluctantly, to spend the day with him visiting his family and church members. He clumsily apologized for "missing out" on my life, admitted that my successes were in spite of and not because of him, and acknowledged what a good job my mother had done raising my sister and me alone. I took responsibility for the intentionality of my anger (Fatherless Woman Syndrome[2]) and how I used it to drive a wedge between us, denying him any opportunity, once I was a teenager, to rectify his wrongs (Boylorn, 2013).

XX

Our relationship is complicated. The absence that started when I was a little girl continues in my adulthood. In many ways his absence forced me to be independent and conditioned me to not need him to be a significant part of my life. Potential male lovers lose interest in me because I have taught myself to take care of myself, with or without a man. The women in my family—fatherless daughters themselves—encouraged me to be independent. I understood their warning to mean that I should not expect or need a man to contribute to my emotional and financial wellbeing, but unfortunately there is no emotional and monetary remedy for fatherlessness or loneliness.

XXI

I hate him for leaving me and not being who I needed him to be. I hate him for caring more about other women than me. I hate him for being unfaithful and unbearable. I hate him for setting me up to be entirely self-sufficient. I hate him for everything he didn't do, and even the things he didn't know (how) to do. I hate him for not being enough to make me feel (good) enough. But I love him with all of my heart. It's a love-hate-love kinda love, with unconditional and unending forgiveness wrapped around my resentment. I can't love anybody else until I love him first.

NOTES

[1] Cliff Huxtable is the fictional father on *The Cosby Show*.
[2] Barras (2002) refers to Fatherless Woman Syndrome as a manifestation of suffering that results from father absence. She discusses five categorical symptoms including 1) feeling unworthy and unlovable;

2) fearing rejection, abandonment and commitment; 3) using sexual expression for attention and affection; 4) overcompensation and overachievement, and 5) unexplained expressions of anger and rage.

REFERENCES

Barras, J. R. (2002). *Whatever happened to daddy's little girl? The impact of fatherlessness on black women.* New York: Ballantine.

Boylorn, R. M. (2013). *Sweetwater: Black women and narratives of resilience.* New York: Peter Lang.

Boylorn, R. M. (2014). A story & a stereotype: An angry and strong auto/ethnography of race, class and gender. In R. M. Boylorn & M. P. Orbe (Eds.), *Critical autoethnography: Intersecting cultural identities in everyday life* (pp. 129-143). Walnut Creek, CA: Left Coast Press.

hooks, b. (2004). *We real cool: Black men and masculinity.* New York: Routledge.

Majors, R., & Billson, J. M. (1992). *Cool pose: The dilemmas of black manhood in America.* New York: Touchstone.

Robin M. Boylorn
Department of Communication Studies
The University of Alabama

ANDREW F. HERRMANN

THE GHOSTWRITER

Living a Father's Unfinished Narrative[1]

According to Goodall (2005) a narrative inheritance "provides us with a framework for understanding our identity through" the stories of those who preceded us in our families (p. 497). Their stories provide context and continuity to help us understand our lives. Ballard and Ballard (2011) supplement the concept of narrative inheritance with the idea of "narrative momentum," suggesting that family identity moves forward into the future through the narratives the family tells (p. 80). In this layered account, I question the hegemony of both concepts.

*

November 2011: The telephone rings loudly in the dark, jerking me out of sleep. As I stumble across the room, I turn on the light, and pick up the phone.

"Hello."

"Is this Mr. Andrew *F.* Herrmann?" says the voice on the other side, emphasis on the "*F.*" It sounds official. Crap.

"Yes."

"Mr. Herrmann, the state of Florida regrets to inform you about the passing of your father Andrew *A.* Herrmann. We are contacting you in regard to his estate."

I bolt awake—eyes wide—shivering in a cold sweat.

That dream.

Again.

I hate that dream within a dream.

*

The dream haunts me every few months, not always when sleeping. Sometimes it flits through my mind in unguarded moments when my eyes are open. I've been having this dream for the past few years, when my mother turned 68. My father, wherever he is, turned 70. I've seen my father once since 1983, for a weekend in 1997. We haven't seen each other, nor spoken since, when he disappeared again (Herrmann, 2005).

*

J. Wyatt & T. E. Adams (eds.), On (Writing) Families, 93–101.

"Leave me alone, because I'm alright, Dad. Surprised to still be on my own."
—The Smiths, 1987

*

My father will not leave me alone. Like others who have (or had) strained relationships with their fathers (Adams, 2012; Bochner, 2012), people say I should try to reconnect. "Your dad is seventy. You should do everything you can do to find him, to develop a relationship with him while you can." I tried reconnecting; it didn't work.

Writing "My Father's Ghost" (Herrmann, 2005) was therapeutic. At the time I realized I'd done as much as I could to find, visit, and reconnect with my father. I understood it was no longer up to me to try to maintain a relationship with a man who did not want to be in a relationship. I let him go. However, given the recurring dream, my unconscious did not. I soon divulge the contents of the dream to my youngest brother.

*

"Maybe that call will finally be a release from the uncertainty, the ambiguity, the frustration of not knowing," Jim says. "After all, wouldn't knowing he's dead be better than all of this not knowing."

"I can't really answer that until his death happens."

"Well there's nothing you can do about it," Jim says.

"I know that, but I'm telling you, the next time I hear about Dad, it will be because he's dead. I'm the oldest. I'll be the one who will have to deal with his shit again. I dread that call. 'We are contacting you in regard to his estate.'"

"Estate?" Jim asks.

We laugh: a laugh with sadness in the back of our throats, threatening to choke us. In this moment, I am reminded of my mother's words. "There is something here that I can identify with, when they reminisce about their boyhoods ... something of a bond ... a horrible bond of loss and sorrow" (Herrmann, 2011, p. 507).

"What estate?" Jim asks, "They want to talk about what he left us? Let's start with depression, alcoholism, self-esteem issues, drug abuse, and emotional distress."

*

Estate. Property. Assets. Wealth. Legacy. Heritage. Birthright. Blessing. Inheritance. That's what we—my brothers and I—are dealing with: narrative inheritance. Narrative inheritance and related intergenerational research into personal identity and family stories is a blossoming point of research (Goodall, 2006; Hunniecutt, 2012; McNay, 2009; Wyatt & Adams, 2012). Many of these tales begin with the death of a parent or intimate partner, a place and space where the author can begin to make sense of the narrative they inherit. Bochner (1997,

2012) writes eloquently about his father's death, both in the immediate aftermath and later as he attempts to come to terms with their relationship. Trujillo (2004) explores the secrets and the silences of his "Naunny." Krizek (1992, 2003) delves into his primary identity and his relationship with his now deceased father in conjunction with their shared love of baseball.

In contrast to these intergenerational narrative and narrative inheritance pieces, our father is not dead, but absent. Our narrative inheritance is incomplete and in complete disarray, because our father lives. Somewhere. We cannot inherit what is not concluded. He still writes.

*

Ramsey Road: A street one block away from our home on Barbara Place. Nanny lived there. Grandma and Grandpa Herrmann lived there. Aunt Margie and Uncle Claude lived there. Aunt Angie and Uncle Nick lived there. Great-grandpa and Great-grandma lived there. Grandpa Herrmann's greenhouses stood there. You couldn't throw a pebble without hitting someone in the family. After Dad left, Mom was frugal. Mom was smart. Mom slogged her ass off—raising three boys, going to college, and working at Head Start at the same time. Without Ramsey Road, that could not have happened. A place of caring, of family, of safety, of love: Ramsey Road.

*

August 2012: As I walk down Ramsey Road, everything seems so small. The property and the houses still stand. The landscaping, paint on the houses, and cars are different. The greenhouses are long gone, replaced with a subdivision. Everyone who lived there now calls the cemetery next to the Bound Brook Presbyterian Church home. Ramsey Road is empty.

As is Barbara Place. There are no children running around the cul-de-sac. No teens riding bicycles. The neighborhood—like me—is older. It is no longer home. I know I'll never return here. Walking back to my car, I hum the lines of a song: "I would rather not go back to the old house. There's too many bad memories, too many memories there" (The Smiths, 1983).

*

Summer 1987: "Andy, there's a phone call for you," my brother Fred says, laying the phone on the kitchen table.

"Hello?"

"Mr. Herrmann, this is Anna Marie Stopher calling from the state of Florida. I'm calling in regard to fifteen thousand dollars in back taxes owed on property in North Fort Myers."

"Fifteen thousand dollars? What?" I'm flustered and flabbergasted. It takes a moment to digest the information.

"Wait, you aren't looking for me, you are looking for my dad, Andrew *A.* Herrmann. I'm Andrew *F.* Herrmann. I'm nineteen years old and just finished my first year in college. I don't own any property."

"I can tell that by your voice," she says laughing. "Do you have information by which I can contact your father?"

"No. I haven't seen or had any contact with my dad since 1983. I have no idea where he is or what he is doing."

"I understand," she says. "Thank you for your time."

She understands? She might be the only one who does. My brothers and I certainly don't.

*

I kept searching for a Father. Drew, my step-father, tried his best to be a father to my brothers and me, but we were hard on him. As my brother Fred says, "We were already all messed up by the time Drew came along." I felt bad for Drew, coming into a single-parent home with a fourteen year old, an eleven year old, and a seven year old. We were cruel, obnoxious. We loved him, but given the trauma of losing his business and our home, our relationships suffered (Herrmann, 2011).

*

August 2012: "When your Aunt Sylvia died a few years ago," Uncle Eric begins, as we sit around his kitchen table having coffee, "Your cousins wanted your father there at the funeral. She was our sister, and he should have been there. They found him and called him. They said they would pay for his plane fare and his room and board while he was here. He turned them down. Over and over he turned them down. I don't know what's wrong with him. Depression. Embarrassment. He's my last sibling, my only brother. No one has heard from him since."

*

I looked for surrogate fathers, pinning my desires on various men over the years. My first philosophy teacher. My Master's thesis advisor. My pastor at River of Life Church. My dissertation advisor. I was searching for someone to look up to. Someone to emulate. Someone to be proud of me. Someone to love me. They never asked for this responsibility, but unbeknownst to them, I laid it at their feet. Nor could I love them the way I wanted to, the way a child wants to love and be loved by his father. Each of these relationships suffered, because they didn't live up to my expectations. How could they? I repeated the same pattern again and again. It took me forty years to realize what I was doing and to break the habit. I was looking to others for a "good" narrative to inherit.

*

September 2012: "Andy, I know your father is still alive," Mom says. "I know this because I was told to check at the local Social Security office every six months or so. If he dies, I'll get more money, because I was married to him much longer than either your step-father or Charlie."

If he dies, she'll get more money. Good. He owes her. He was a deadbeat dad twenty years before "Deadbeat Dad" became a part of the common American lexicon in the 1990s. A little more money in retirement to make up for the money she didn't get when my brothers and I were kids. To think, I may get a call about my father's death from my mother, rather than the State of Florida. Why does she have to be burdened with that responsibility? She cleaned up enough of his mess.

*

I sit at my computer and type "Andrew Herrmann" in the search bar. My finger hesitates momentarily over the return bar. I have been here before. I stare at the screen. My hand moves away from the return button. I close the browser window. I cannot do it this time. This scene repeats.

I have hit the return bar in the past, and when I do, numerous "Andrew Herrmanns" are found. I scroll through them.

Maybe that's him. Nah, couldn't be. He'd never live in New Hampshire. Maybe that's him. Nope. Too young. Maybe that's him. Nope. That's me! Is that him? Age: 70. State: Florida. City: Tamarac. That is probably him.

"Come on Andrew. Aren't you done with this? He doesn't want a relationship. He's proven it."

"Are you sure you are looking for him so you can have some contact? Or so you can get your father's love?" I ask myself. "Or are you looking for him to find out that he is dead?"

"Do you never go any further than a web search because you're just afraid and don't want to be rejected again? You don't want to be like an old dog—an old dog that gets kicked over and over every time he returns to his master."

"Yeah, but old dogs eventually learn not to go back. Me? I'm still tempted."

I close the browser window. I feel like Art Bochner: "A man wants to love his father; I know I did. But your actions made it so difficult and confusing" (2012, p. 169). Of course, my father is still alive and a part of me does still want to love him and be loved by him. As much as I want us to be finished business, we remain unfinished, and this is "a difficult fact to live with" (Goodall, 2005, p. 498). My brothers and I have an unfinished narrative inheritance. Our father lives.

*

According to Ballard and Ballard (2011) narrative momentum occurs in all families, passing down the narrative inheritance from one generation to another. Narrative momentum carries the family forward from the past and into the future impacting the family identity through the narratives that the family tells. My brother Fred and I cannot experience narrative momentum through our lived experience. We are both in our forties, unmarried, and childless. With no children to pass a narrative on to, there's no narrative momentum. Like the placard on Harry Truman's desk read: "The buck stops here." While narrative momentum theory is appealing, it is also hegemonic. It discounts the variety of family constitutions and family narratives. It ostracizes the childless. It disregards the parentless. It supports and reinforces the dominant cultural discourses of what defines "family."

Jim's son is fourteen and has no narrative from this paternal grandfather. My nephew never met—and most likely will never meet—Andrew A. Herrmann. What story would my brother tell? About how our father got his three children stoned for the first time on the way to see Cheech and Chong's *Up in Smoke*? About how his second wife almost killed us while she was driving intoxicated? About how he disappeared? Narrative momentum—a narrative legacy—doesn't exist here. This will be gap, a silence. While personal narrative writers and autoethnographers suggest that we look for silences in narratives that are told (de Freitas & Paton, 2009; Poulos, 2010) this silence is an untold narrative itself. Perhaps my nephew will one day "return to what is not known about [his] distant relatives and reopen those narrative museums regardless of any warning" (Goodall, 2012, p. 208). I wonder what my nephew will think of what he finds there.

*

October 9, 2012: I'm sitting on my couch, writing the first draft of this essay, when I pick up my ringing telephone.

"Andy." It's Charlie, my mom's husband. "Andy, I want you to know your Uncle Neil died this morning. Your cousin Nick was there at his side and your cousin Dina was on the phone at the same time when he passed." We talk about arrangements, cremation, possible visits.

They were together. That's good. My uncle was estranged from his children for many years, but over the last few years, with a lot of work and patience, they patched things up. They visited. They reconnected. He met his grandchildren. In the end, he was able to pass a good narrative down. This news brings with it a realization: my aunt's and uncle's generation is passing on; my mother's generation; my father's.

*

Somewhere behind the scenes, invisible to us, is our father the ghostwriter, composing his narrative. In the process, he is writing what we will inherit. Perhaps my brother James is right: Our father's death will end his narrative, and if that ending is not neat and clean—if that narrative doesn't bring a sense of completion—it will bring closure.

I keep my phone close.

NOTES

[1] This article is dedicated to the three men in my life who passed away in 2012: Neil Abbondante, Bud Goodall, and Nick Trujillo.

REFERENCES

Adams, T. E. (2012). Missing each other. *Qualitative Inquiry, 18,* 193–196.

Ballard, R. L., & Ballard, S. J. (2011). From narrative inheritance to narrative momentum: Past, present, and future stories in an international adoptive family. *Journal of Family Communication, 11,* 69-84.

Bochner, A. P. (1997). It's about time: Narrative and the divided self. *Qualitative Inquiry, 3,* 418-438.

Bochner, A. P. (2012). Bird on the wire: Freeing the father within me. *Qualitative Inquiry, 18,* 168-173.

de Freitas, E., & Paton, J. (2009). (De)facing the self: Poststructural disruptions of the autoethnographic text. *Qualitative Inquiry, 15,* 483-498.

Goodall, H. L. Jr., (2005). Narrative inheritance: A nuclear family with toxic secrets. *Qualitative Inquiry, 11,* 492-513.

Goodall, H. L. Jr.. (2006). *A need to know: The clandestine history of a CIA family.* Walnut Creek, CA: Left Coast Press.

Goodall, H. L. Jr., (2012). The fatherland museum. *Qualitative Inquiry, 18,* 203-209.

Herrmann, A. F. (2005). My father's ghost: Interrogating family photos. *Journal of Loss and Trauma, 10,* 337-346.

Herrmann, A. F. (2011). "Losing things was nothing new": A family's story of foreclosure. *Journal of Loss & Trauma, 16,* 497-510.

Hunniecutt, J. (2012). *Infidelity and identity: Cheating parents, cheating partners, and cheating selves.* Paper presented at the National Communication Convention, Orlando, FL.

Krizek, R. L. (1992). Goodbye old friend: A son's farewell to Comiskey Park. *Omega, 25,* 87-93.

Krizek, R. L. (2003). Ethnography as the excavation of personal narrative. In R. Clair (Ed.), *Expressions of ethnography* (pp.141-51). Albany: SUNY Press.

McNay, M. (2009). Absent memory, family secrets, narrative inheritance. *Qualitative Inquiry, 15,* 1178-1188.

Morrissey, S. P., & Marr, J. (1983). Back to the old house. [Recorded by The Smiths]. *Hatful of Hollow* [CD]. New York: Sire.

Morrissey, S. P., & Marr, J. (1987). A rush and a push and the land is ours. [Recorded by The Smiths]. *Strangeways Here We Come* [CD]. New York: Sire.

Polous, C. N. (2010). Spirited accidents: An autoethnography of possibility. *Qualitative Inquiry, 16,* 49-56.

Trujillo, N. (2004). *In search of Naunny's grave: Age, class, gender and ethnicity in an American family.* Walnut Creek, CA: AltaMira Press.

Wyatt, J., & Adams, T. E. (2012). Introduction: On writing fathers. *Qualitative Inquiry, 18,* 119-120.

Andrew F. Herrmann
Department of Communication
East Tennessee State University

KITRINA DOUGLAS

GOING HOME[1]

Stories do not merely narrate events. They convey on action and actor—
either one or both—the socially accredited status of being worth notice. To
render narratable is to claim relevance for action, and for the life of which
that action is part. (Frank, 2004, p. 62)

In *The Renewal of Generosity*, Arthur Frank (2004) reminds us that storytellers
continually redraw boundaries, and "render present what would otherwise be
absent" (p. 62). In this chapter I would like to "render narratable" a brief moment
that has been hidden or perhaps, to put it more succinctly, has been silenced and
lost among other stories that have been invited, shared, or created publicly about
me and my family during my sport career.

My purpose for sharing *Going Home* is that within sport culture the following
stories are often accredited the status of *unworthy*. For Burke (2001), Halbert and
Latimer (1994), and Madill and Hopper (2007) this is unsurprising given what is
valued in sport lies within a very narrow narrative script, one that is hegemonically
masculine, and "promotes strength, power, war metaphors, and deemphasizes
healthy lifestyle choices … and appropriate social interaction in society" (Madill &
Hopper, 2007, p. 45). Accordingly, the stories I share have *become* unworthy due
to the interests of "gatekeepers," the media and others who "expand some rhetorics
while ignoring others" (Plummer, 1995, p. 119). By this I mean, because these are
not stories about winning a tournament, achieving success, or about being tough
and strong, nor are they stories about conquering my fears, overcoming the enemy,
or rising to a *worthy* challenge—the *stuff* that fills sports pages of newspapers, they
have been ignored.

Frank (1995) has shown a narrative type to be "the most general storyline that
can be recognized underlying the plot and tensions of particular stories" (p. 75).
Within elite and professional sport, three narrative types have been identified: the
performance, discovery, and *relational* narratives (Douglas & Carless, 2006). The
performance narrative conforms to media representations of a worthy story; its
focus is winning. For athletes who align with the performance narrative,
performance-related concerns infuse every area of decision-making, life, and
identity. Further, each dimension and phase of life is considered by how they
impede or enhance performance. However, even those people whose experiences
and body fail to align with this plot have their lives judged by the values of the
performance narrative—and *that* plot still gets *into their heads*. The theoretical
backdrop to this essay therefore is to understand how this powerful and dominating
narrative influences people in sport.

J. Wyatt & T. E. Adams (eds.), On (Writing) Families, 103–114.

The record books detail that at the Wirral Caldy Classic (Cheshire, UK), a golf tournament on the Women's European Tour, I withdrew after the first round citing an injury as the cause. My friends remember going to collect my clothes and other belongings as I didn't go to the hotel after playing. Instead, I drove home. The medical records at my local General Practitioner's (GP) practice show I was provided with confirmation from a GP that I was unable to perform that week. This is an account of these events. Through two stories I hope to show how the "expected" narrative plot in sport can motivate an athlete to question her "self" and how others' questions can motivate a parent to question what she knows about her daughter and their relationship.

GOING HOME

The feelings started long before she got to the golf course, but she wasn't sure exactly when, or why. There was something, and it didn't go away. She knew, at least thought she knew, she didn't want to be *there*, she didn't want to play.

It wasn't that she was playing badly, but she wasn't playing particularly well either. It wasn't a course she particularly enjoyed, but she didn't particularly dislike it. It wasn't a major tournament, but it wasn't an insignificant tournament either. It wasn't a cold, wet or windy day, and goodness knows links courses can be wild and windy at times, but neither was it particularly hot and sunny. It was, however, the most perfect time of day for her, an early start. There were no groups in front to slow her play, no spike marks to hamper the roll of her putts towards the hole, no footprints in the bunkers, the greens were freshly mown and fast, the air crisp, the breeze yet to rise, and yet, what her body told her, was to go home.

"On the tee representing Mizuno," the starter announced. She nodded and raised her hand toward the crowd thanking them for their applause in acknowledging her achievements. She hit an ok drive, an ok shot to the green and a couple of ok putts. At the second hole she got a birdie, which should make her happy, shouldn't it?

uprising
tears welled,
vision clouded
I want to go home

> *No, wait, masquerade*
> *for the crowd*
> *Act professionally*
> *You're a pro,*

A pro who doesn't want to play
today,
this feeling
I am engulfed, swallowed
why am I still here?

        this is your job,
        it's how you earn your living,

Yes, but, I don't want to
be
here

        you'll be home in three days' time
        it's hardly a long time,
        and you've paid out a lot to be here, travel, entry fees,
        you need a return on your investment,
        you need to win
        money

Yes, but I hope

        Don't say it

I miss the cut[2]

        You can't say that, you never miss cuts

But, this was day One; the cut was way too far off.

I think I might
Walk in

        Don't be silly

Why? Why stay

        You're not allowed to leave an event,
        the tournament has been sold based on the top players
        playing, and
        it will affect your order of merit position,
        and
        that will affect what you get to play in next year,
        and
        you've got responsibilities, colleagues, your sponsor,
        the tour, the fans who pay to
        watch you,

Yes, I know, but I really
don't want

        You're probably just tired, played too much,
        burnt out

Yea, so shouldn't I go home

        No, not yet,
        after the event, for now

just try to cover costs,
cover your feelings
and what if you did go home,
what are you going to do there,
and what if next week
you don't want to play either

Well, then I won't go

And what if that happens again
What if it keeps happening

Then I'll stop playing

What about all your talent?
Goals left unfulfilled
There'll be plenty of time to be at home
When you're old
How would you earn a living?

I'd do something else

Have you any idea
what something else
is like,
how many people would give their right arm
to do what you do,
have your lifestyle
see the things you've seen
be able to do what you can

Yes, I know,
but if I don't want to be here

And the income,
you won't get decent money
working in…

Yes but

tears
another shot,
another putt
the tide going out
and never
never never
coming in
life
a wilting flower
starved of water

By the fifteenth hole she'd made up her mind and formulated a plan. At the end of the round she would sign her card, and then leave, just go home, and not tell anyone her plan, so the do-gooders wouldn't try to change her mind, or over sympathise. She didn't want to explain. She didn't want to talk. She wouldn't need to change her shoes, she'd driven in her spikes before, she would put her clubs in the car, and just drive, drive home.

The next hole dragged, but she felt a little better knowing she had a plan.

tread water,
three more holes,
Show no fear
two more holes,
smile at the crowd
one more hole,

She came off the course, went into the scorers tent, signed her card, and she was away.

released,
action
flow
air

Three and a half hours later she walked into her home.

"Hello," her mother said, slightly surprised, "Didn't expect to see you till Sunday." And they slipped into mundanity. No questions, no lengthy explanations, discussions; well, there was one question:

"D'you want a cuppa?" her mother asked after giving her a big hug, "the pot's just made, I'm taking mine in the garden" and with that her mother walked on with her cup of tea and a slice of cake, "Those weeds are up again and" her voice trailed out of earshot as her mother wandered into the garden.

*

The sign read, "*Give your name to the receptionist and take a seat.*" Which she did; waiting for the buzzer to sound and flash so that she knew it was her turn to see the General Practitioner.

"I need a doctor's note," she said to GP. She sounded authoritative.

"I see," the man said, reading her notes; they were very, very short.

"I'm obviously not well." The words stuck in her throat.

She had a problem saying she was *ill* partly because she felt happy and healthy, so what illness was she claiming? Homesickness? Travel sickness? Sea sickness? Love sickness? Motion sickness? Depression? Burn out? At that moment, when she was claiming her illness, in a dimly lit room devoid of sunshine, on a plastic covered chair, in front of some greying, pale GP, she didn't know, exactly; everything about her body exuded life. Her appearance was very healthy, relaxed, sculpted, muscled, strong, fit, tanned, money in the bank, a supportive family, and a close loving boyfriend. What was it that was wrong?

Nothing
A big fuss
Do you realise the money you are wasting?
Don't you think doctors have better things to do?
Have you seen the sort of lives people lead
who come to their GP with problems?

Her word wasn't enough for the tour. She needed proof. This man could provide the proof. He was authorised to give an account of her life.

It's a lie,
the note,
so you don't get fined
for walking off for No Reason!

Crying
on the golf course
isn't normal
is it?
That happened
Didn't it?

She hated being there, enclosed in his *sick* room, needing this man's authority on her decision. But the tour required proof: if she was unable to play golf, a doctor's note was needed to withdraw from a tournament or a player would be fined. In her head the words were clear. This was her diagnosis, not the doctor's. He nodded, scribbled a note and that was that.

CAUGHT IN A SCRIPT WITH NO WORDS: A MOTHER'S STORY

"Kitrina," she interrupted, as only a mother would. Then she wandered over to the ringing phone, put one finger to her lips and lifted the receiver. It was her father, "Hello Daddy," she said. Until that moment her daughter had been merrily blasting *I'm Forever Blowing Bubbles* on the Hammond electric organ. She loved the way her daughter filled the house with sunshine, and she loved the way her daughter's music filled the house with life. She'd been so pleased to have her home, but, at that moment, the bubbles were a little too much for her. Her daughter, it seemed, had taken her words "daddy" to mean it was *only* her grandfather and she could return to "pretty bubbles in the air," this time with a rock beat selected, "bum-bum pretty, bum-bum bubbles." Like many mothers, Pauline thought it best to just find another space rather than dampen the enthusiasm she saw in her offspring. So she escaped the onslaught of bubbles by walking to the kitchen and left her daughter singing at the top of her voice in the sitting room.

She could now hear her father clearly.

"I said," he continued after being told to "wait a minute," "shall I drop those pots down or are you coming up?"

"No, I'll pop up" she replied, "I've got to do some shopping in the village anyway." Pauline continued.

"Ok, that's great," he said, then, "when does that talented daughter of yours get back?"

"She came back yesterday," Pauline replied.

"Oh! That's early, how did she get on?" he asked. The question caught his daughter by surprise.

"Ugha?" bought her a few seconds to consider, but, when she did consider it, she surprised herself, "I don't know." As the words came out of her mouth, she was suddenly aware of the humour of it and had to stifle a little chuckle. It was a *James Bond* movie moment, and she was the dumb blonde. She was happy to see her daughter home. Before her daughter left they didn't fuss over details like *when will you be back, what time will you be in*—though she was aware other parents did. When she saw her daughter she was just pleased to see her, she gave a big hug and they had tea and cake in the garden. She had cajoled her daughter into helping with the weeding, and they both became captivated by the most glorious setting sun over the Bristol Channel. Even though she knew her daughter hated her watching *Coronation Street*, she'd stolen away to catch that evening's episode while her daughter got her pastels out and recaptured *their* sunset on paper. Later in the evening they ate dinner together; it was a lovely, lovely evening. Her father interrupted her thoughts.

"What do you mean you don't know!" he questioned, this time in a more aggressive tone, rather confused by Pauline's ignorance about his granddaughter.

"Well, I didn't ask her, she didn't mention it and we were busy with other things," she tried to explain quite unapologetically, unemotionally, and rather offhand, thinking back to the previous evening's fun.

Her father wasn't a violent man, but, over the years, she had experienced some of his more angry moments. This seemed to be heading towards one.

"You don't know!" he carried on, "That's terrible! She'll think you are totally uninterested and don't care about her. How can a mother not know how her daughter finished in a tournament? For goodness sake Pauline, I can't understand your attitude! Don't you care?"

Surprised by the sudden bombardment, she ended the conversation abruptly, making an excuse of needing to take a sauce off the boil, then hung-up the phone. But his words stung, and then, like a stench, began to infuse, dissolve, and erode what she thought she knew about her daughter and their relationship. His words threatened to fracture something so special. *"Perhaps I had got it wrong?"* she thought. *"Should I be asking more questions about where she finished in the golf event? Should I care more about the result? Where she is in the ranking? Should I ask more questions about the next event? What type of mother am I?"*

REFLECTIONS

Narrative truth, Ellis and Bochner (2000) write, "helps keep the past alive in the present" (p. 745). I would like to discuss three motives that provoke me to keep these stories alive.

Challenging the Performance Narrative

I have become increasingly aware of the insidious nature of the performance narrative. And it's not just coaches, ministers of sport, and performance directors[3] that story life in sport through the performance narrative script, a script where performance concerns take precedence. Outside of narrative or feminist colleagues, almost every person I speak with, and this was especially so during the UK's hosting of the Olympics, seem to accept uncritically that athletes *have* to be a particular way in order to win. That is, athletes *have* to be single minded, *have* to sacrifice other dimensions of their self and life, *have* to put their training and performance needs first, and *have* to dedicate their lives, body and identity exclusively to their sport—in order to win. Yet, in the research that David Carless and I have conducted over the past decade, some athletes' stories lead us to question this monological and totalitarian narrative. That is, not all athletes value winning (see Douglas & Carless, 2006); some athletes story life in sport as a journey where it's "whom you make the journey with" that is important, not the ultimate destination (Carless & Douglas, 2012). Other athletes have suggested, for example, that winning is only like getting a note for doing homework and what makes life meaningful is discovery, in the form of travel, learning about new things, wine, flowers, food, or becoming a parent (Carless & Douglas, 2009; Douglas & Carless, 2009). Other athletes, through sharing alternative stories have helped us understand that sometimes we (athletes) are expected to tell a story, that is far from how we experience life in sport and far from the story we would prefer to tell (Carless & Douglas, 2013; Douglas & Carless, 2009), and as I have experienced, sometimes the stories we tell are just ignored and deemed unworthy. Missing from the public narratives are stories like this essay, where an athlete walks away from competition to enjoy other actions, playing an electric organ, singing at the top of her voice, or watching the sun set with her mother—and the acts being documented as a good thing, where the athlete isn't "wasting" her talent or jeopardising her career.

One purpose of including the trip to the GP and my grandfather reprimanding my mother is to show how difficult it is to tell a different story about sport (Gilbourne, 2012). The culture we live in, as McLeod (2007) suggests, provides an ill-fitting template. When an athlete deviates from the expected narrative script, their lives and stories are policed back on course by shepherds whose aims are to "help them reach their potential."

Counterstories, like this, not only keep the past alive for the storyteller, but keep future possibilities alive for others (Holman Jones, 2005; Zanker & Gard, 2008).

A Living Testimony

A second reason for sharing this particular story is as a testament to one type of relationship a woman might develop with her mother. For narrative theorists, an individual's ability to sustain an alternative story is largely due to alternatives types of stories being available and valued (McLeod, 2007). This suggests that what my mother facilitated was the opportunity to narrate action, and from it, create potential to develop an identity unrelated to golf performance. By *not* asking where I finished in the tournament and, in contrast, by inviting me to "pick raspberries," "do weeding," "take tea," and so on, she made it possible to create alternative— non-performance-related—stories. On the golf course and in press interviews these alternatives may have been mentioned, but they are largely missing from reports that were published. While the media and others in sport culture were shaping my "public" identity in a singular way, at home, multidimensional identities were able to be developed. To me, this underscores the importance of making alternative stories available for parents, not just athletes.

Hearing the Body

My third reason for sharing this particular story is related to David Carless' and my on-going research interests attempting to tease out and explore the limits and boundaries of narratives (Carless, 2010, 2012). By this I mean, in recent years we have followed others and began to question what goes unsaid because of the limits of language. In the process of writing songs, for example, we have been sensitised to how our bodies respond to rhythm, the tonal vibrations of a guitar, to music and how these communicate something long before a narrative plot is made known. David Carless' (2010) work on sexual identity has also shown how bodies have the capacity to interrupt and derail narratives. He writes,

> I have come to appreciate through reflecting on my own experience: that the personal stories we tell, based as they are on broader narratives that circulate in our culture, exert a powerful influence on the actions and inactions of our bodies in the world. Our bodies, however, "talk back" to this process because bodies have an existence beyond stories. Embodied experiences have the habit of intruding, and then intruding again, on the personal stories we create of our lives. (p. 342)

In the first story, two narrative maps were placed side by side, to stay or go, but the discussion brought little resolution. What settled the matter wasn't a clearer, more logical or truthful argument. Rather, as David Carless suggests, it was the body *talking back, intruding, and intruding again.* On the golf course, away at a tournament, there was something missing from my body and only going home, it seems, would fill that void. I suggest these are the types of things we know in our bodies. I have no proof for this, only what my body feels. And of course I am aware of many arguments for why I shouldn't trust my body, my memory, or my trickster stories (Frank, 2010; Freeman, 2010). Yet, there was

111

some*thing* that made it possible for me to walk away from the golf tournament and resist the extremely powerful dominant narrative to stay and compete. If, as Madill and Hopper (2007) suggest, athletes are encouraged not to live a healthy, balanced life, it seems these are the types of stories that may help us understand what a healthy choice is and how to take it. But I wonder, when and how, in the milieu of modern sport, do we help young people listen to the body and not the "No pain, no gain" stories?

In the second story my mother also decided to act in a way that is counter to the dominant narrative. Yet, she was unable to account for herself/action to my grandfather. His script, his story, expected her to ask where I finished in the tournament and/or if had I won. What my mother did was hug me. Then she invited me to take tea in the garden. This is the script, the story, that I want to hold on to, and what makes going home an experience worthy of narrating.

POSTSCRIPT: STILL SHARING A COUNTERSTORY

Two women sit in a blue painted beach chalet on the Cornish coast. The patio doors are wide open and the curtains blow gentle in the afternoon breeze. In the distance the Godrevy lighthouse stands proudly lit by the afternoon sun, as a new swell arrives to temper the dark jagged rocks and the golden shoreline.

One woman sits chuckling to herself—she's sending text-messages. The other, brow furrowed, sits across from her typing on her laptop. She is responding to reviewer number one, who tells her to "write more honestly," that she "can't address an audience in a performance," and that she also "shouldn't direct rhetorical questions to an audience." She's annoyed; the other three reviewers were captivated by the performance. She speaks to reviewer one in her mind: "I am writing honestly," she tells him. Suddenly her thoughts, conversations, and internal arguments are interrupted.

"I love my iPhone," the first woman announces loudly, and laughs again. It's a hearty deep laugh, and her entire body wobbles.

While the second woman knows she's been interrupted, and something has been said, she didn't actually *hear* it. But she stops, allows her mind to fish for the words and draws their meaning toward her. Once they land on her shore, she tastes, feels, and repeats them in her mind, *I-love-my-iPhone.*

As the words are slowly digested, she realises she has just been nourished by a counterstory. As if a dew-drop had landed on her forehead, this 84-year-old woman sitting opposite her—her mother—had not only derailed her thoughts but, more importantly, had derailed a dominant narrative about aging, a narrative which goes along the lines of "an old dog can't learn new tricks." She recognised this because that's the type of research she does. She recognised, at the same time, that her parents continually offered her counter-narratives when she was younger that made it possible to resist the dominant narrative in sport. And she recognised, in that moment, that her mother is still making a way forward for her, paving the way if you like, away from a negative future story that she may be sucked into. Women of 84, you see, aren't supposed to be able to learn computer skills in their eighties, especially those who left the work force at 23 to start a family, women who spent their lives "bringing-up" children, always being there. They are supposed to be *past* being able to develop skills which might allow them to access up-to-date-modern-gadgets, and as for actually, "loving" them. But there she was. *Her* mother had provided *her* a counterstory to slip into her pocket, for later use. To quote her singer-songwriter friend, her mother put "a rainbow in her pocket" for a sunnier journey. She felt love and admiration towards the woman who sat laughing, who perhaps had no idea of the gift she'd just given.

She then realised that the announcement a few moments earlier, *I-love-my-iPhone,* was meant to invite dialogue and so finally she asked:

"Why is that?" looking over and away from the trivia that had previously held her gaze.

"I just got a text from Jessie," said the 84-year-old.

Jessie is the 84-year-old's granddaughter, born when she was 67, her first grand-daughter.

As her daughter pondered all of this she also became aware of two other things. Firstly, in order to tell a counterstory, her mother required her children and her grand-children to play their parts. That is, these "others" had to allow her not to be cemented in one identity so fixed in their minds that she couldn't grow, develop, and change even in her 70s and 80s. Channels had to be opened to allow someone who has never used a laptop, iPhone, iPod, to value what they bring and not draw on an "I'm too old for that" story.

Then, she also realised that her mother's interest in the "gadget" wasn't just about being "up-to–date," "with-it" or different. Even though she said, "I always liked gadgets," her daughter reckoned the main use of this "thing" was that it allowed her mother to be touched by and to touch those she loved when she was unable to physically touch them, hold them, and hug them.

In that moment too, with all these thoughts whirling in her mind, the daughter felt sadness, her eyes became cloudy. She knew one day her mother would be out of reach, unable to physically hold her, and she wondered if telling this story would be a way to reconnect, to reach out, and be held.

NOTES

[1] I would like to thank the editors for inviting me to contribute a chapter to this collection. This opportunity provided me with a way to make worthy little things that get omitted but give my life its meaning. I would also like to thank David Carless for being a sounding board, listening ear, and a gentle breeze, and Kim Etherington for bringing sunshine and encouragement.

[2] In professional golf the first two rounds are played by all of the professionals who enter the event. Then, after two rounds the field is divided into two groups. The top 60 players (or 40, in smaller events) continue, and these players are paid depending on their position. Those outside of the top 60 are "cut" from the event and usually receive no money.

[3] David Carless and I have discussed at length elsewhere how the performance narrative is used to frame what is expected of athletes. We reference the Minister for Culture & Sport, who suggested he would "change the culture of sport in the UK," the Director of the Australian Institute of Sport, who suggested on a BBC documentary that "winning" was the "sole" focus of the AIS. We also reference our research with coaches who showed a lack of understanding for any narrative that failed to align with the

performance narrative. Further discussion of these points is beyond the scope of this chapter but can be found in Carless and Douglas (2013) and Gilbourne (2012).

REFERENCES

Burke, M. (2001). *Sport and traditions of feminist theory.* Unpublished Doctoral Thesis, Victoria University, Victoria, Australia.

Carless, D. (2010). Who the hell was *that?* Stories, bodies and actions in the world. *Qualitative Research in Psychology, 7,* 332-344.

Carless, D. (2012). Negotiating sexuality and masculinity in school sport: An autoethnography. *Sport, Education and Society, 17,* 607-625.

Carless, D., & Douglas, K. (2012). Stories of success: Cultural narratives and personal stories of elite and professional athletes. *Reflective Practice, 13,* 387-398.

Carless, D., & Douglas, K. (2013a). Living, resisting, and playing the part of athlete: Narrative tensions in elite sport. *Psychology of Sport and Exercise, 14,* 701-708.

Carless, D., & Douglas, K. (2013b). "In the boat" but "selling myself short": Stories, narratives, and identity development in elite sport. *The Sport Psychologist, 27,* 27-39.

Douglas, K., & Carless, D. (2006). Performance, discovery, and relational narratives among women professional tournament golfers. *Women in Sport and Physical Activity Journal, 15,* 14-27.

Douglas, K., & Carless, D. (2008). Using stories in coach education. *International Journal of Sports Science and Coaching, 3,* 33-49.

Douglas, K., & Carless, D. (2009). Abandoning the performance narrative: Two women's stories of transition from professional golf. *Journal of Applied Sport Psychology, 21,* 213-230.

Ellis, C., & Bochner, A. P. (2000). Autoethnography, personal narrative, reflexivity. In N. K. Denzin & Y. S. Lincoln (Eds.), *Handbook of qualitative research* (2nd ed., pp. 733-768). Thousand Oaks, CA: Sage.

Frank, A.W. (1995). *The wounded storyteller.* Chicago: University of Chicago Press.

Frank, A. W. (2004). *The renewal of generosity: Illness, medicine, and how to live.* Chicago: University of Chicago Press.

Frank, A. W. (2010) *Letting stories breathe: A socio-narratology.* Chicago: University of Chicago Press.

Freeman, M. (2010). *Hindsight.* Oxford University Press. New York.

Gilbourne, D. (2012). Contemplations on sport, complexity, ages of being and practice. *Sports Coaching Review, 1,* 4-16.

Halbert, C., & Latimer, M. (1994). "Battling" gendered language: An analysis of the language used by sports commentators in a televised coed tennis competition." *Sociology of Sport, 11,* 298-308.

Holman Jones, S. (2005). Autoethnography: Making the personal political. In N. K. Denzin & Y. S. Lincoln (eds.), *Handbook of qualitative research* (2nd ed., pp. 763-791). Thousand Oaks, CA: Sage.

Madill, L., & Hopper, T. (2007). The best of the best discourse on health: Poetic insights on how professional sport socializes a family of men into hegemonic masculinity and physical inactivity. *American Journal of Men's Health, 1,* 44-59.

McLeod, J. (1997). *Narrative and psychotherapy.* London: Sage.

Plummer, K. (1995). *Documents of life 2: An invitation to critical humanism.* Sage: London.

Zanker, C., & Gard, M. (2008). Fatness, fitness, and the moral universe of sport and physical activity. *Sociology of Sport Journal, 25,* 48-65.

Kitrina Douglas
Department of Exercise, Nutrition and Health Sciences
University of Bristol

JANE SPEEDY

DYING IN THE CARE OF THE NHS

Fragments From a Daughter's Love Song for Her Father

Over recent years I have become interested in critical, performative ways of "remembering" and in so doing, in deconstructing the spaces and entanglements betwixt memory, identity, time and narrative. This chapter takes the form of a performance text in three fragments, and comprises a layered account (Ronai, 1995) that splices snatches of newspaper articles and television programs, jazz pieces, memories, obituary, journal extracts, and photographs. Together this "scrapbook" of sliced and layered texts provides sideway glimpses of my father's last days, and of our shared sense of humour and relationship with each other. This text speaks to many meanings of "care" and to many ways of creeping "under the radar" and out of "the gaze" (skills my father taught me well)—even in our dying.

FRAGMENT ONE: WATCHING THE TELEVISION NEWS, NOVEMBER 15, 2009

Dad's had a chest infection and is tired from all of the coughing, so we are just sitting quietly playing "spot the bigot" with the television, which is not hard today as Barack Obama's speech about health care ("Obama-care" they are calling it over the pond) has been liberally spliced by the BBC[1] with sound bytes from "middle America."

"Look at this one, look at this one," Dad splutters excitedly. "This one's going to be *appalling*, you can tell by his hat."

"Well, not necessarily," I say. "They've got a whole different thing going on with hats over there. Michael Moore[2] wears a hat like that, for instance."

"Shhhhh, listen ...."

"This is the tip of the secular socialist iceberg that is going to lead to the moral and financial ruin of the United States of America. I just hope and pray that the good lord can find another country in which to carry on his work... "[3]

"Blimey!" exclaims dad. "It's the Pilgrim Fathers. I knew we should have nuked the Mayflower on its way out of Plymouth harbour back in the seventeenth century when we still had the chance. Look at all the trouble they're causing now."

"Mmm ... you must admit though, Dad, that was articulate bigotry. You wouldn't catch George W. Bush coming out with a phrase like 'the tip of the secular socialist iceberg' now would you?"

"Well, no its got two three-syllable words in succession for a start...It is amazing though ... How can the same country that elected Obama—I mean that's

J. Wyatt & T. E. Adams (eds.), On (Writing) Families, 115–122.

such an intelligent move—how can they *not* want a decent healthcare system, I don't get it!"

"How could they *not* want all of this?" he continues. "Here I am, well past my 'sell by' date, but I'm in being looked after by the NHS[4] in my own home. I have nursing care every few hours, doctors on standby, all this flashy equipment on permanent loan—and enough medication to get myself disqualified from the Olympics several times over! How could anybody argue against this?"

*

But perhaps we should go back a little bit, because although they didn't know it at the time (on November 15, 2009), this was one of the last conversations the father and daughter would ever have. Perhaps we should go back to a time a little earlier, perhaps a few days earlier, while the father was still in the hospital.

FRAGMENT TWO: NOVEMBER 10, 2009

It is a long, complicated cross-country journey and his daughter arrives at the hospital in the evening. She has come on various trains, straight from work, trailing a suitcase, a briefcase and various shopping bags along behind her.

He is asleep, as he so often is these days, in the arm chair next to his bed, pen in hand, *The Guardian*[5] on his lap opened at the quick crossword page. She pulls up another chair and as she waits beside him, she finds herself taken back some thirty years or more …

The Porth Lisky Headland, St. David's, Pembrokeshire

Memory: A Sunny, Slightly Windy Pembrokeshire[6] Day; Their Spot on Porth Lisky Headland; July 1973

He's leaning against the rocks with his legs sprawled across the soft, springy grass. She is at a right angle to him, lying with her head resting against his legs, her knees drawn up to make a resting place for her folded newspaper. They are doing *The Guardian* quick crossword. She inputs each word and he is (mostly) the clue-solver. They have a system, which is strictly adhered to. First the down-words and then the across-words; to do otherwise is inconceivable.

She can smell heather, wild thyme, and sea pinks and although she is looking directly into the sun and cannot see them, she can hear skylarks above and seagulls chattering and squabbling on the foreshore.

Dad does not need much help with the crossword clues. He is making quick work of it, but then she gets two inter-connecting clues in quick succession: "MEAN PINBALL" and "PINBALL WIZARD."[7]

And he is surprised and somewhat bemused.

November 10th, 2009 (Continued)

He is awake now in the hospital and chatty, eager to tell her his news.

The radiotherapy has made no difference at all it seems, apart from making him feel a little queasy.

Today had been the last day of his treatment. The young consultant's eyes had filled with tears, he reports, when she told him that nothing more could be done, that this was how life would be from now on…but it did not really matter as much to him as it had seemed to matter to her.

"I'm old," he said, "and I'm just wearing out. They can't cure everything and I have everything I need."

"As long as I have the use of my hands to hold a book or a glass of wine and if I can still read and listen to music then I'm fine. I've got all I need these days and at least now I can't feel any aches and pains in my legs any more."

He does not say: "I'll be alright until it creeps up into my brain—that is what I'm dreading."

He does not say that, but quietly turns and looks out the window and so she shows him how to work the iPod she has brought him. And he is delighted and astonished that she has managed to get so much of his favorite music as well as several talking books onto such a small gadget.

She leaves him sipping an illicit gin and orange from his tooth mug, plugged in, listening to his current hero, Barack Obama, reading his life story.

*

But of course he was only in the hospital for quite a short time that occasion. It all happened so quickly at the end. Perhaps we should wind back to the weekend just before this when, on her visit, he woke up in the morning unable to move?

FRAGMENT THREE: OCTOBER 31, 2009

I am sitting here beside you as you sleep: Your great shock of white hair flopping out all over the pillows. You are propped up against a mountain of cushions, waiting for the ambulance to come. You are exhausted.

We found out this morning that more tumors have been sneaking furtively up your body and, unbeknownst to us, have taken up residence in the bones of your back, somewhere in-between your shoulder blades.

Here they have shamelessly settled into extending their influence outwards, pressing down on every nerve they come across as if they own the place. This is why you have lost the use of your legs overnight and are unable to feel anything below the waist.

In a long line of indignities and confusing experiences over the last couple of years, this feels like one blow too many.

*

Let's return to the scene in the bedroom on November 15, 2009, around the time when we entered this story, where a daughter sits at the end of the bed, watching quietly over her elderly father. His elderly wife is downstairs, distracting herself with an assortment of domestic tasks.

Then he wakes up and she, the daughter, plays him jazz from her phone "swinging the berries," from the original Emmett Berry[8] post-war Parisian album "boogie-woogie à la Parisienne." His face lights up, widening into a glorious grin when we get to the tenor saxophone solo.

This might have been the moment to have whispered "I love you" or kissed the top of his snowy white head. But she did not.

She did not because she did not want him to know that she knew (even though she knew he knew) that he was going to die soon. So she played him jazz and he grinned and metaphorically tapped his paralyzed feet.

This was their love song.

*

I have packed your hospital bag with clean pajamas, dressing gown and slippers, the money to buy *The Guardian*, the Sunday Times book of the 100 most difficult Sudokus, pens, razor, washing kit, glasses case, spare catheters, wipes and tissues, two Mars bars and an innocent looking bottle of freshly squeezed orange juice, liberally spiked with Plymouth Gin.[9]

This is my love song.

Memory: Selham Church, 1970

They had not been particularly close when she was little, Jane and her father. It had always been like the Ladybird "Peter and Jane" books: "Chris helped Daddy mend the car, while Jane helped Mummy do the washing up."

Then when she was about thirteen, Jane and her father bonded over "Jack Smith's architecture project" at school, during which time they had spent weekend after weekend together touring the ancient churches of Sussex, from Ditchling to Didling, on their bikes. Selham church was one of the oldest, and the smallest, in the country. They cycled over to Selham together in the spring of 1970, towards the end of Jane's work on her project. By the time they got over to Selham, they'd got their way of working together off to a fine routine. First they'd wander round the outside, Jane making notes and consulting her textbooks, looking up everything she saw—and Mick taking photographs. Then they'd tackle the inside the same way, always in complete silence. Unless of course, somebody had left the church organ unlocked, in which case Jane would feel that it was only right and proper to have a little tinkle on the ivories. Selham church possessed an unlocked wheezy Victorian harmonium, on which Jane treated her dad to his favorite of her "party pieces"—the theme tune from the television series *The Virginian*, and he treated her to her favorite of his "party pieces" his "Gary-Cooper-strolling-down-main-street-ready-to-draw" walk from *High Noon* down the aisle of the church, ducking and weaving between the bullets that were flying down at him between the pews. Later they propped up their bikes against the west wall at the end of the church and sat on a couple of nearby grave stones to eat their picnic lunch, over which they broke their code of silence. He said he'd taken loads of photos of the snakes carved into the chancel arch[10] and she said she'd thought that they were nothing special because they didn't even appear in her book on Saxon church architecture.

"Maybe that's because they're so rare," he'd suggested.

She'd said nothing out loud, but had just thought to herself, "If it's not listed in the book, it's not listed in the book, you know-all."

The next week at school she had told Jack Smith that she had been to Selham Church.

"Fabulous," he said. "Isn't that the one with the mystery carved arch?"

"Yes, what is it?" she'd replied.

"Nobody really knows," said Jack.

"Could have been taken from some earlier Viking building, or perhaps from some much earlier pagan place of worship that was already on that site. It's certainly several centuries older than the rest of the church."

"Well I took a lot of photos of it," she volunteered, her face reddening.

Thirty years later, as a professor of qualitative inquiry methods, she regularly advised her research students to take "textbook methods" and "textbook thinking" with a pinch of salt.

"Who taught you to read texts in such a way?" students would often ask.

"My Dad," she'd always reply.

Selham Church near Midhurst, West Sussex

FRAGMENT THREE: OCTOBER 31, 2009 (CONTINUED)

You cannot get out of bed, let alone down the stairs, and so paramedics strap you to a canvas trolley, trundle you out into the square and onto their ambulance. We climb in with you and travel to Canterbury, a violently bumpy journey in what is apparently Kent's oldest ambulance.

Georgian perhaps? Is there such a thing as a grade two listed ambulance?[11]

By the time we arrive you look and feel sick, but we are ambushed at the hospital entrance by the monumental ward sister for accident and emergency who appears to be moonlighting within the National Health Service from her regular job as an Easter Island statue.

"Can't be done sweetheart," she insists. "We can't admit you here, there are no beds, we're going to have to turn you away."

"But my General Practitioner ..." the father begins.

"Oh the GPs always say that," she interrupts. "If there's no beds, then there's no beds."

His shoulders sag and his elderly wife looks tearful. Dave and Claire from the ambulance service shift awkwardly from foot to foot.

The daughter moves swiftly round the stretcher to stand next to the ward sister and leaning forward, asks if she could have a quick word. She speaks quietly, but there is something fiery and resolute in her eyes. They step inside the lobby and, although it's impossible to catch what they are saying, it's easy to see that the ground is shifting, that there is something happening in the space between them.

The daughter stands quietly where she is whilst the nurse goes back inside the building. They all wait. Silent. Motionless. And then the ward sister reappears. She brushes past the daughter and opens up the entrance doors.

"There's a bed," she says.

As he glides past her onto the ward the father grabs the daughter's hand and pats it. She smiles.

This was her love song.

POSTSCRIPT

This chapter was submitted for publication to the editors (Jonathan Wyatt and Tony Adams) on November 7, 2012, the day after the USA re-elected Barack Obama, the last in the long line of Mick Speedy's political heroes, for a second term in the White House. Mick's daughter Jane had routinely watched David Dimbleby's[12] *American Election Night Special* on BBC television in the company of her father. In 2012 she watched (nearly) all seven hours of it through the night, by herself. Her partner found her at seven o'clock in the morning, curled up on the sofa, in floods of tears, sitting watching Obama's victory speech in Chicago. "*The best is yet to come*"—a great speech—Daddy would have been so pleased, so very pleased and proud. He would have loved to have seen this ..."

Mick Speedy at his First Wedding (May 1948) and at his Second Wedding (October 1998)

121

JANE SPEEDY

NOTES

[1] British Broadcast Corporation.
[2] Michael Moore is a documentary filmmaker from USA and director of the film *Sicko* which compares European, American, and Cuban systems of healthcare.
[3] Quotation from Newt Gingrich's (2009) book.
[4] National Health Service.
[5] The centre-left national British newspaper.
[6] The most western county in Wales.
[7] *Pinball Wizard*: The defining song by Pete Townshend, from the 1969 rock opera *Tommy*, performed by the British rock band The Who.
[8] Emmett Berry, 1915-1993, African-American Jazz Trumpeter from Cleveland, Ohio, who played with many of the traditional Jazz greats such as Count Basie and Billie Holiday.
[9] Plymouth Gin, distilled in Plymouth since 1793, reputed to be the preferred gin of the British navy.
[10] http://www.crsbi.ac.uk/search/county/site/ed-sx-selha.html
[11] Buildings "listed" (in grades one, two or three) by the British government are considered as being of special historic or architectural interest.
[12] The BBC's most distinguished political television journalist. David's father, Richard, had been and his younger brother Jonathan remains, BBC political journalists. Thus, members of the Speedy family had been watching members of the Dimbleby family reporting on European, British, and European elections for more than 50 years.

REFERENCES

Ronai, C. R. (1995). Multiple reflections of child sex abuse. *Journal of Contemporary Ethnography, 23*, 395-426.

Jane Speedy
Graduate School of Education
University of Bristol

GUNNHILDUR UNA JONSDOTTIR

TEMPORARY BLINDNESS

SHE TELLS ME HER DREAMS

Series of endless mornings merge into one. It is dark outside, winter covers the sky and brings us more rain than snow. Rain that makes the sky look blacker than black, like a thick veil of oily wetness. The outside is one, blurred with water and darkness. Inside, by the kitchen table, me and my mother. Radio voices whisper in the background; she is wearing her terry cloth robe and I sit by the table. Dressed. Eyes heavy with the dreams of a night that is barely passing. Sound of cutlery and dinner plates while my mother empties the dishwasher. There is a story on the radio, a children's story. Sometimes I listen, sometimes I simply enjoy the monotone voice, as a humming of an ocean, or a quiet river. She sits down by the table. Also blinking her eyes trying to bring focus to the reality of being awake. She tells me her dreams. I tell her my dreams. My dreams become stories, linear, sometimes taking place on multiple lines simultaneously. Sometimes there is just this one person, or a feeling that I remember. Through the voice of my mother, the voice emanating from the radio, my own voice is formed. In my mind. It has no sound, only presence. We share the dreams without listening too deeply to each other. We both know it is about telling. Not so much about listening. We still listen. Then the day starts.

*

We are together side-by-side, darkness wrapped around us, creating a path towards the place between sleep and awake. Voices become shapes turning into paths that we were able to walk by, one step here and there. Dreams are reality, feelings shared by turning stories from another into our own imagination. The moment, our action which has no clear goal, our voices becoming part of a murmur from the radio, it all bears the signs of us being beset by the abject. We share words, as if in a conversation, but truly we have no definable object of conversation. The "I" from the radio is an equal participant of this conversation without an object. There is no desire for meaning, the dreams are entering the morning without a purpose. Yet the telling of the dreams might fascinate desire as it is drawn toward an elsewhere. Were we indeed haunted by the abject, literally besides ourselves (Kristeva, 1982)?

*

J. Wyatt & T. E. Adams (eds.), On (Writing) Families, 123–129.

Radio, mother, child. Voices recounting dreams and radio stories around them. Sound has no body; it mixes like vaporized material, three sources of sound, one reality created within the kitchen walls. Dreams. Which reality is mine and which is hers, is there but this only one, where we have never been together? Or have we? Again, if we are the ones by which the abject exists, we are dejects. We face two or more places: the place and space of our dreams, the place and space of the kitchen, the place and space of the story created by the radio voice. Thus I ask these questions concerning my place: Where was I? Which place was reality? Was reality more than one, one space but many places? Or one place but many spaces? I, as the deject, am still astray, on my journey, constantly aware of my danger. My only comfort comes from Julia K., who promises me that the more I stray, the more I am saved (Kristeva, 1982).

*

Now, years later. I am the mother. I sit in the kitchen with my child and we tell each other our dreams. The same space is recreated as I move clean dishes from the dishwasher to the shelves.

*

We look awry, sounds of cutlery, steel creating cling clang cling clang, silver bells sounding as from the secret dance of the Twelve Sisters (Grimm, Grimm, & Tatar, 2004). The twelve sisters who disappeared from the castle every night, leaving no trace of evidence but their worn out dancing shoes to be found each morning. As if it all happened in a dream, but the object of dream-action had found its way into the dawning reality. *The Worn-Out Dancing Shoes.* Is there an object of our dreams created in our stories? Do we make the dreams real by recounting them? Can nothing indeed beget something (Žižek, 2000)? A dream told in the morning, never quite real but based around this trace; the story. Can a dream take on a form of the object in our otherwise abject experience as non-subjects, only half-present? Floating through physicality we never doubt each others' experiences. Dreams are the true mornings.

TEMPORARY BLINDNESS

She holds my hand. The accident had been in the afternoon of the day before. Sitting in the passenger seat of the car, I felt the road swing upwards, away from the ground, and throw the car over, into the sky, rolling and crashing down. I only remembered the first roll; after my head hit the ground through the side window I saw nothing. Darkness. Confusion. The pain was constant, sharp knife in my back with every move, every breath. Hurting skin, the little cuts feel like a thin coat of slight but constant burning. For years after I see a grain of sand embedded in the skin of the back of my left hand. In that point, little black dot, I am one with nature. Back, wrist, head, neck. Broken, cut, bruised. I have long dark hair then. My scalp is bleeding, full of the black sands of the South. Trying to wash this sand away, I bend over the bathtub side, attempt to hold the shower-head and rinse my hair with one hand. Screaming with anger. I have to get help. The other hand is in a cast. The cast over this left hand which later becomes a symbol of my sadness. The hand that could not play the piano as before. Along with my back injury, my identity as a piano player is erased. I was almost eighteen. My mother helps me. She holds my hand. Silently, making a shushing sound with her voice.

*

Trauma. Physicality, identity, broken, broken neck, broken back, broken arm, grain of sand, a moment. The moment of the trauma has defined me. No longer a promising young piano player, now a young adult with a broken body. I was never quite able to face this change of identity. I always thought I would "get better." I always thought that then...then...then I would play the piano again. This moment defined me without my realization. In this moment I grew up. Becoming a woman, bleeding from unusual places, the head, the wrist, the arm. Not the becoming of a woman that took place much earlier, with bleeding from the usual places. This red liquid that is either normal or abnormal to lose. Normality depending on exit places from the body. Our body. My body. The broken body.

*

Where does the broken body become the only one? Do I remember my unbroken body? Does anyone have an "unbroken" body? What happened that day? Do I really remember it so well? Or is it storytelling, recreated every time I tell it?

*

Our physical being in the world. For me the hands had a special importance: piano. My head injury in the crash caused me to lose consciousness, but when my mind woke up again, my eyes did not function. Temporary blindness. I heard voices; a stranger was by my side, talking. Calming me down. I felt my eyes open but was in the darkest darkness I have ever entered. Blind. In fury I started negotiating with a potential God: "—God, if you are there ...—God, listen ...—God, please, anything but my eyes. I have to be able to read the sheets of music." I promised this potential God that I would accept being in a wheelchair, if only he could let me see. Wheelchairs can be rolled to a piano, I thought. Such was my reasoning. In a moment of trauma. My eyesight returned but my inner blindness became more than temporary. This moment visited me twenty years later. In the hospital. Fear. Realization. I am not getting better. I never asked my parents about how this felt to them. Their daughter, broken. Did they have the same anger as me? Did they have the same instant connection to the piano? Did they feel anything, when I was in the hospital twenty years later dealing with suicidal depression? I never asked.

I REMEMBER

In Maurilia, the traveler is invited to visit the city and, at the same time, to examine some old post cards that show it as it used to be: ...If the traveler does not wish to disappoint the inhabitants, he must praise the postcard city and prefer it to the present one, though he must be careful to contain his regret at the changes within definite limits: admitting that the magnificence and prosperity of the metropolis Maurilia, when compared to the old, provincial Maurilia, cannot compensate for a certain lost grace, which, however, can be appreciated only now in the old post cards .... (Calvino, 1997)

Why do I tell my stories? Why to I suppose they are true? Will I upset someone? By describing a reality that they have lived a different version of? Who is right then? Shall I ask permissions? Permission to present my own reality?

*

Reliability of our memory has been shown to be influenced by the emotional impact of a given moment, creating a difference in how our brain treats traumatic memories compared to the vast collection of other memories (Van Der Kolk, 1998). Writing autoethnography I find myself confronted with challenges. I am uncertain about the "truth" of my memories, and I have hesitations about describing situations involving other people, my friends, my family. My parents know that I am writing but I am not comfortable with including them in the process. There are some delicate confessions here. Probably the reader will not notice, but I do.

The accident is different. I find myself compelled to ask, at least to offer them to share with me their experience as they remember it. Through this I realize even more clearly how my personal memory of the accident is defined by the trauma. I remember details, voices, physical experiences; the back door of the ambulance. The days around, immediately before and after are however blank. I have no clear memory of them.

My question of the truth of my memories has created a longing for remembering "accurately." Browsing through my bookshelves I gather everything I find which could possibly deal with memory. I know that the art of memory has a long history (Yates, 1966). Memory and the longing to keep the connection to what we believe to be "truth" also brings us closer to the beginning of this chapter, creating reality through telling my dreams.

HANDS

My father's father, my grandfather had died. It was in my late teenage years, those years while I was furious at my father for most things in life. Dead body in a coffin. One by one people make a gesture with their hand. The place has low lighting, perhaps there was something shining through a stone glass window. I hear a murmur of shushing sounds around me. People moving quietly. Whispering perhaps. Some farewell words or some religious words. I was next to my father in line. I cannot remember who was in front of whom. I had spent years fighting and proving that I was a big girl. A woman. When I took my step towards the coffin I became a little child again. Without thinking I reached out and grabbed my father's thumb. Not his hand. He has big hands. Big and beautiful hands that build things. Mine are also big, but long and narrow and they do not build things. They draw images and make music. I reached out and grabbed his thumb. I held onto him like a rope from a life raft. I did some of the hand gesturing as was expected and my father probably did something similar. We walked away from the casket. I let go of his thumb. We never spoke of it.

HOME TO THE WORLD OUTSIDE

I am a mother now. Three little children, jumping, running, playing. I return home after spending a week in the hospital. I had wanted to die so my children could get a better mother. It was discarded as stress of the modern times and I do not talk about this idea of dying to anyone else than the medical staff. This is my first submission to the hospital and my first time returning home. Home, to the "world outside." I am afraid. Afraid of everything. Places, spaces, objects, words. I am scared when I open the door to my home. My husband at work, children at school. Baby Julia is now with me again. She is too little for school, and my father has taken care of her; my mother is still working.

*

When saying goodbye, my father tells me that now I have had time to rest, but the others have been taking care of things for me. It was now my turn to take care of things myself. I am slow to react. Not until he has left and I am alone with baby Julia do the words start having an impact on me. "Time to rest," I hear him say. "Time to take care of my responsibilities."

*

I hear that I have been absent. I am struck with guilt. An absent daughter. An absent mother. Selfishly depressed. My responsibilities had to be handled by someone else. My children were taken care of by someone else. Today I can revisit this memory and understand that I had not failed. That it is quite ok that my family took care of my children while I was ill. But at that time I did not see myself as being ill. I do not explain the unspoken idea of "removing" myself from the family by suicide, to create space for "a more qualified" mother. I am silent. I sit at the kitchen table and say good-bye to my father. I am now home. Taking care of my children. The daunting feelings of failure jump, run and play within me.

127

*

My father's words. I heard them as judgment. That I had failed. That I had burdened everyone. That I had been on "holiday," resting. Absent while others took on my responsibilities. I am afraid. I don't want him to be angry at me. I don't know if he was. Sometimes these little nuances of how we hear create ideas that were never said or believed. Still the impact is the same. As if he thought I had now, once again, gone too far. Selfish. That he thought I was selfish. This is an old problem for me. I think my father thinks I am selfish. I cannot talk about it.

*

I slowly float through a couple of days, numb and unprotected. I start to be afraid again. I cannot find safety anywhere. I see things that are not happening. I am afraid. Afraid of everything. Terrified of myself. Terrified of the seduction of the images of horror. The soothing whisper that promises peace through death. Feeling of sharp scratches of an imagined rope by my neck becomes like a soothing gentle touch of a loving hand.

*

I am in the kitchen with my daughter. My older two children are in preschool and first grade of elementary school. We are alone. She, laughing, playing, so self-confident. So fearless. So certain about the kindness of the world. I see a butter knife. An image of blood fills my view, gushing red blood originating in my wrists. I blink. There is no blood. My heart beats and I am almost paralyzed with fear. I carefully push the butter knife out of sight. Under the bread. She laughs and I am there, but so helpless. I cannot face her. I am so afraid that she will see how scared I really am. That I am not strong enough to take care of her. That, if something happens, I am not enough. We sit there, by the kitchen table, me and my daughter. She is happy with her morning snacks. I try to look the other way. I don't make a shushing sound with my voice.

MOOMINPAPPA'S MEMOIRS

Again I sit down at my kitchen table. Again baby Julia is with me and again my father has driven me home from the hospital. For the second time. This second time I stayed longer. Faced my illness and started to accept help. I was so burdened by guilt, being away from my children. Not being able. Unable to take care of them in a crisis. Until I gave up. I stopped crying over my dinner plate every night. I started to read *Moominpappa's Memoirs* by Tove Jansson. I laughed out loud while I was reading. Such a relief to feel the use of those facial muscles again. Slowly I get ready to go home. Now facing the illness. With a smile. Perhaps a little bit forced, but still a smile.

Again I say goodbye to my father. Again he speaks to me on the way out. My father tells me that everything will be all right. I hug him. He is big and warm. He tells me to be careful, to call for help if I need it. There is no mention of me having gotten rest while others took on my responsibilities. We both know that I am ill. Still weak after the hospital stay but yet so much safer than before. My father. He is there. I am there. Present.

We discuss the reasons for the hospital admissions. Mostly when we are in the car, alone together. He is driving and I sit in the passenger seat. We are going to the land of my little cabin; he is going to help me with something. We talk. We keep up an unusually long and sincere conversation. We talk about my great grandmother. Just a few words. We mention my great uncle. If it can be true that he developed schizophrenia after a head injury while working on a fishing boat. We talk about the bipolar. We joke but we both know the pain. Outside the front side window I see the lava fields, rough stones covered in a thick layer of soft moss. Gray or green. Moss should be green, one thinks, but this moss is gray.

*

Facing illness. Weakness. Talking about the unspoken. Ancestors and us, same people through the same fears. Fear of oneself. Bipolar, schizophrenia. Joking about pain. Humor to approach the unspeakable. Landscape as the security of home. Color as a backdrop for creating variations. Memory of landscape as a space for conversation.

Was I once again at my kitchen table? I don't remember. But my baby, Julia is there, smiling. The older children are there too. Smiling. I thought I would really have to work on making them happy again, after this summer of unexplained trauma and mental illness. I discover that there is no need for that. When I am happy, they are happy. Even if I am still afraid. The fear will take years to settle.

But I can handle the butter knife without losing control over my breath.

REFERENCES

Calvino, I. (1997). *Invisible cities* (W. Weaver, trans.). London: Vintage.

Grimm, J., Grimm, W., & Tatar, M. (Eds.). (2004). *The annotated Brothers Grimm.* New York: W.W. Norton.

Jansson, T. (1969). *The exploits of Moominpappa: Described by himself.* Middlesex: Penguin Books.

Kristeva, J. (1982). *Powers of horrors: An essay on abjection.* New York: Columbia University Press.

Van Der Kolk, B. A. (1998). Trauma and memory. *Psychiatry and Clinical Neurosciences, 52,* S52-S64.

Yates, F.A. (1966). *The art of memory.* Chicago: University of Chicago Press.

Žižek, S. (1991). *Looking awry: An introduction to Jaques Lacan through popular culture.* Cambridge, MA: MIT Press.

Gunnhildur Una Jonsdottir
PhD Student
University of Iceland

SOPHIE TAMAS

BEDTIME STORIES

1

In the moonlit park, dew glistens on my shoes. The dogs are pale orbiting smudges. I dial my mother's cell phone. No answer. My phone rings in my pocket a moment later. I could not find my phone in the back seat, she says. I was returning your call, I say. Oh, she says, I was just checking in, a motherly call because yesterday you were weeping. Oh sweet jesus. A reflexive chatter of reassurance, as if that could undo the compulsion animated when my partner told her that I was having a hard day.

I had in fact been howling—head in hands, elbows on counter—worn out by steering relational dynamics off the shoals of frustration and producing elaborate family meals; by my three teenage daughters' reluctance to help my parents weed and stack wood and my partner's resistance to doing his manly domestic duties; by my desire to be outdoors instead of at my desk and their dithering dawdling departure to drive our eldest back to school. I was undone by a gush of despair. Abandonment issues. I cried for a long time. This is not what I tell my mum.

2

My only sibling lives abroad with his wife and two little boys. Before one of their very rare, very brief visits I write to him. I am angry that our mum has worked so hard to welcome a prodigal son who will only stay a few days. His boys are adorable strangers. I miss him and feel hurt. I say so, and then some. Is he avoiding the conflict of closeness or did our ties get sacrificed in the complex cross-cultural negotiation of his marriage?

A few days later I pick up my dad at the airport and mention the letter as we turn onto his street. You might want to know, I say lightly. I heard, he says. Your brother's wife phoned your mother in tears. He shakes his head, muttering, the less I know about it the happier I'll be. Well, I say, I learned tact from your Genghis Khan school of social work.

Days of waiting for blowback, heavy with dread. My mum returns from meetings in NYC. She does not call. I think she is mad at me. Why don't you call her and ask? my partner says. Squeeze that pimple. No, I say, sometimes they just dissipate if you leave them alone. The fist in my chest is not a problem that I can fix.

J. Wyatt & T. E. Adams (eds.), On (Writing) Families, 131–139.

The phone rings while we are having sex. I assume it is my dad; who else calls at 9:05am on a Wednesday? I call their house. Did you call? No, Mum answers, voice wan and flat. Did Dad? Maybe. I'll check. He did. Goodbye.

My brother and his family arrive. It is the best visit we have had in years.

3

My grandfather has no eyelashes now; just soft folds of skin around creamy eyes that once were blue. They focus on my face, an arms length away.

Can you take your pills? It takes a while to cross ninety-three years at the speed of sound.

Yes. Pause. Why do I sound so …?

You're weak because you haven't been eating and the lying down is affecting your lungs. Soon as we get this nausea under control and get you moving you'll get your voice back.

I kneel beside the bed, sippy cup ready, pills on my outstretched palm. Today he can drop them in his own mouth. He closes his eyes to drink. I'm like a baby, he says, shaking his head in disgust.

Maybe for now, I say, smoothing white wisps of hair, but a big, wise old baby. He laughs, then blinks, eyes wide and pupils small. He touches one of my long curls. I never noticed your hair before, he says. It's a helix.

My mother's mother sits in her mother's grey cashmere cardigan, fiddling with the rubber bands that hold white ankle socks on the handles of her walker. The saddest sound I ever heard, she says, was singing at two in the morning. We all went to the windows. There was a group of German prisoners of war, being marched up the street to the barracks, and all of them were singing—she hums the tune until the chorus pulls the name up from the deeps—Lily Marlene. You know it, don't you? I nod, my hands busy with potatoes.

They are astonished by what I accomplish in a day, and cannot imagine that my life at home runs even faster. I kneel over their beloved cat, grateful it only has half its teeth as I coax pills down its gullet and shoot it, twice daily, with insulin. Every couple of hours I prepare small dishes of mild foods that stick to a spoon and present them to Gramps with plucky persistence, making everything okay by sheer force of calm competency.

Hello baby, I whisper into the phone, in my grandparents' basement, under the covers, past midnight, my course prep set aside. My partner launches into an account of his hard day with our girls, but it pours through me in a muddy flood. I have no space to contain it; I am filled with my grandparents and the awful inevitability of their absence. What will remain? Looms and spinning wheels and carving tools I don't know how to use; tableware for courses no longer served; generations of obsolete small appliances. Memorial objects dispersed like DNA among the family they live for. I want to ask my grandfather, if energy can neither be created nor destroyed, where are they going?

My mum has arrived so I can drive six hours home to teach at the university. Grampa is swaddled in a recliner, dozing in front of Cirque du Soleil. So, I say leaning over him, no carousing with loose women, no getting drunk, no partying all night. A long pause. Then what is left for me? he asks, without opening his eyes.

How is he doing? I ask.

We'll get the x-ray results on Wednesday, Mum answers, her voice close and distant in the speakers of my van. I am following the taillights ahead through the snow and dark.

Are you okay? I ask. Oh yes, she lies. Just tired. It was a hell of a week.

I can come back on Tuesday, I say, to spell you off.

We'll see, she sighs. That might be good.

I come back for reading week. You have done so much for us, Grampa says. I did not want to ask you to come but we could not have managed without you. It takes courage to ask for help, I say. I am glad that you did. It is your job to say what you need and my job to decide if I have it to give.

When he is well enough to try driving, we go to the bank. I carry a tin that once held a bottle of Scotch and now is full of loose change. I pour it into the coin counter and bring him the receipt. Three hundred and eighty dollars! he says. You'll have to go on a date, I reply. The pretty bank teller serving him smiles. Sounds good to me, she says. I'm free tonight.

While we wait for assistance in the cell phone store he tells me about the tracks that ran along the shore of Lake Ontario near the place where he spent his boyhood summers, and the box cars that paused there in a lay-by, and the hobos he met riding the rails during the Great Depression, and the conversations he struck up with them, and the totem pole one man whittled and gave him as the train pulled away. He kept it for years. I do not ask where it went. Like all things will be, it is lost. When the story ends, I teach him how to send photographs as text messages on his iPhone.

After supper, my grandparents are sitting at the kitchen table, in mismatched rolling office chairs, sorting pills and papers. I am facing them, across the counter, washing dishes. Gran says, did you say your ex is moving back to Almonte?

Who? says Gramps.

Joe, she says, louder. And that your mum is going to let him into the house? Who?

Even louder. She is going to let Joe into her house for Baha'í.

Why?

For Baha'í things. It's a small community I suppose.

Gramps turns to me. He's Baha'í?

Well, I say, on paper.

But I thought they weren't—

It's like priests, I shrug. Some of them molest little boys, but still call themselves Catholic. I smile, suppressing the thrum of shame that marks unspeakables.

She's letting him into her house? Gramps continues.

I nod. The girls don't want her to, I say. It's one of their safe places, but if he's there, it's … Another shrug.

But what about your Dad? Surely he …?

Gran interjects. Maybe *she* rules the roost.

Either of them could say no, I explain. But they won't. Hospitality is a big part of their faith. And it's community gatherings, so.

Well, Gran says. I would NEVER let him into my home.

No, Gramps shakes his head. Nor would I.

I feel both comforted and sad.

4

Our eldest is approaching the end of her second year at university in a small city six hours away from home, near the gated senior's colony where my grandparents live. I call her after class; she is feeling great, she says, better than she has felt in a long time. A few hours later her roommate looks up my middle daughter on Facebook, and she, in turn, sends us a text message. Our big girl is in the hospital. I was there several weeks ago with Gramps, while he had pneumonia that I may have caused by over-medicating his post-op pain. I knit and watched him sleep or plied him with apple fritters and frank conversations, my feet up on the end of his bed and a germ mask dangling from one ear. The staff were responsive and kind. The emergency mental health unit is not like that. I do not like to think about her long smooth legs splayed out on the bed, her shirt riding up to show a soft slice of hip above her cotton panties. I cannot sort out how many hands and where they held; if they left prints on her thighs, a thumb shaped bruise on her calf as she kicked. When tickled, she flails wildly. Was it like that, with no laughing? She tells us she screamed, what are you putting in my body? as the needle bit. We were not there.

My partner drives all night. He finds her cowering, unrecognizable, surrounded by little piles of paper obsessively filled with the fragments of her epiphanies.

Her panic subsides once they let her place calls. I am standing in the kitchen as the words rush out: I had a thought I wanted to share and you are the person I want to share it with first. I need to find it. I just need to write things down and then all the feelings I never had words for, if I am talking on the phone and writing at the same time, all the words are there, and I can say everything. I can finally understand everything. I just need to remember so I write it down. I love you, she says, tell the girls I love them too. Promise.

Okay, I say. I will. I love you too. She tends to forget this, to withdraw, abruptly, sometimes for weeks. After nine years living as a full-time blended family her trust wounds remain unhealed. All of us have broken pieces, with sharp edges that can scrape. She has recently been more demonstrative. Is that part of the mania? What does love mean when you're crazy? Is there any other kind?

My partner calls. The tears climb up from his sternum, hooking their spikes in each rib. I was getting her clothes from her room, he says. I started shaking too bad, I had to leave. I could not find—he is sobbing now—her soft pants or the shirt she wanted or anything, it is all dirty and all over the place. If you go to the store, I say, call me when you get to the panty rack, I can tell you what kind to buy.

He got off on the wrong foot with the nurses. They didn't like the look of him—bearded and broad with a big belly. Then he lay down on the foot of her bed because his back was sore and she wanted him close. The nurse came thundering in, yelling that it was inappropriate to lie on his daughter's bed. I find that very disturbing, our girl yelled back. Are you implying that I have a sexual relationship with my father?

I keep asking them to tell me the rules, he said to the resident. The young man shrugged. They can't, he said, there are too many.

Every day at two o'clock when he is allowed into the locked ward he asks if he can talk to the doctor. He's busy, the nurses say, but you can leave him a message.

I feel positive about my diagnosis, she says. I will finally get the right treatment. She thinks she will be okay, but none of us know how okay will look.

After the first week she is sent to the psychiatric facility across the street. He goes back to work and I spell him off. The younger two come with me, and we all spend an hour together before he takes them back home. They are shocked; this earnest, hyper-sensitive person is someone the sister they know would have mocked. Are all of these versions of her equally (un)real? Who will be left once her brain has been chemically disciplined?

For two weeks I visit every afternoon. I do not know who she needs me to be; my presence is both stressful and reassuring. She gets a day pass and we have supper with my grandparents; she chats readily but does not say goodbye to them and balks hard when I ask her to do so. I say, I don't care what your diagnosis is, your life will not go well if you don't show people basic courtesy. Silence. Must be nice, I say, to be the centre of the universe. Oh my god, she says. I can't have this conversation. That's what you always say, I snap, but other people have needs too. It is her nine o'clock curfew. Once she is gone I sit in the van and sob.

She is discharged. Her lease ends soon; she intends to go tree planting then spend two months at home. We go to pack up her room but she curls up on the bed, cradling the bear I bought her in the hospital gift shop. I assess and adjust expectations. Here, I say gently and firmly, put the bobby pins in the tub. I find loose pins on her shelves, under the bed, in the bottom of her nail polish bin, and put them in front of her, on the duvet. When she is done I take them away and pass her a plastic travel case to refill with q-tips. She lines them up in perfect rows, one by one, with no gaps.

Although she has lived for months in a sty all her things must be sorted before I can put them in boxes. If things are not sorted she will not know where they are and then things might get lost. So we gather all of the earrings in a baggie in the jewelry box, and separate the hairclips from the lip balms. She carefully considers which bracelets to store until the fall, which to send home with me for the summer, and which to keep with her while she camps in her empty room and attends outpatient programs.

I cannot remember the last time that doing things felt this possible, she said, earlier, as we moseyed through a morning of errands that wore her out. It has been so long that I cannot remember, she added, not even in high school.

What should we do, my grandparents ask, if she comes asking for help? Don't rescue her, I say. She is still learning what she can manage, and needs to have clear experiences of cause and effect. She has the right to make her own choices, even if I have my worries about them, just the same as you two can choose things that worry your kids.

Three weeks later, she comes home. She is and is not herself. The medication leaves her calm but disengaged, infused with an optimism that could be a symptom of her disease. I am irritable. You're so angry with her, my partner says. You really outsider her, you don't treat her the same as the other girls. This rankles. The difference is not that I am angry, I retort, it is that I am not allowed to be. The truth is, our love is sometimes anxious, lacking an early foundation in touch; I am not always sure of my place in her. Another truth is, his care for my bio daughters feels like a movement toward me but his care for her can sometimes feel like a movement away; I am that insecure. A therapist who has seen us all says we are the highest functioning blended family that she knows. This is not always good enough, but we are each working hard to mend and maintain connection.

5

The five of us are having supper with my parents. My mum is tired from a week abroad performing religious duties. I was raised to see this as her privilege. The girls are laughing about how our eldest came back from first year and scolded us for being too mean. I agree, says Mum, with marked intensity.

We're just more honest, says the youngest.

The banter continues. Well, I say to Mum, you get the kids you deserve. I point at my dad. That's what he said to me.

She is not amused.

A bit later we are discussing the impact of my kids living in one place for their entire lives. We count up how many schools each of us attended. I am the winner at ten, not counting universities. No wonder you didn't have any friends, the youngest jokes.

You had friends, Mum says.

Sophie, you did have friends, Dad repeats, firmly.

Sometimes, sure, but there is a difference, I say, between friends and a collection of losers huddled together for protection. I remember really awkward birthday parties where you guys would invite kids who did not even like me.

They look concerned. We each have our chosen narratives. Do they understand how my kids float in a constant cloud of significant relationships, sharing clothes, secrets, games, conspiracies and cuddles? They have grown confident in a familiar, stable world, where nobody is really hated, and you are never a stranger sitting alone. They belong here, in this white small town. Every childhood has its cost.

6

I dithered all morning: go to the cottage with my dad and the girls or stay home with my partner and work. They leave. I call a few minutes later: I miss my people, I say. Can you come and get me?

All the way there I second-guess. We spend the afternoon making friendship bracelets. The eldest naps, then wakes. She starts reading aloud, half way through *Oryx and Crake*, a novel by Margaret Atwood. She pauses to explain its dystopian feminist themes to her sisters, and does not feel belittled by my smile. After supper I sit nearby finishing a bracelet for my mum while the girls wash up. They discuss, with relish, their school teachers' quirks and pathologies. I do not chastise them for being harsh. They are tying themselves to each other, working out the pattern. I am the safety pin holding the end of the bracelet, a silent stabilizing witness, connecting the women they are becoming to the girls that they have been.

7

My grandfather's health has improved. My grandparents make an unprecedented trek to our small town, staying in the accessible suite my parents built for them five years ago. The girls prepare a three-generational mother's day meal. Afterwards, we crack open fortune cookies. The game, I explain, is to add the words "in bed" to the end of your fortune. Gran immediately reads her fortune aloud and snickers over the saucy turn. Mum protests the impropriety, weakly, but soon blows tea out her nose laughing as my dad reads his fortune—"Value quality over quantity in bed." Gran giggles all night, tacking "in bed" onto random sentences.

8

My partner and I go to an academic conference, leaving the girls on their own. I discuss with a colleague the possibility of having another baby; it has been on my mind lately, since I gained the job security to make more reproduction financially viable. I want to see our genetic mix, what we'd get if we built one from the ground up. I am forty-one; it is magical thinking and stupidity. But, my friend says, children are always a terrible idea, rationally speaking. I need to decide what kind of wealthy I want to be. I spot babies at the conference, squalling in cloth pouches like hairless marsupials. The mothers seem harried. Will any of them have four kids? I would have to give myself over again to another being without resentment. I would have to trust my partner—recently incapacitated by vicarious trauma—and let him be the main mama in his own way. How could I even consider doing this? Do I have that much life left in me?

But how could I not? Parenting is the most generative kind of suffering, an endless lesson in uncertainty and failing well.

9

We had a great time while you were away, the girls report. The eldest, as planned, left for treeplanting. But by then, they say, she was like her old self. We were afraid we'd never be able to talk again like we used to. And can we get a copy of *Oryx and Crake*?

I read the weather report for her area every day.

10

I attend another academic conference, in Europe. Afterwards, I spend four days in my brother's home. I laugh when I see his cutlery, a painted bird, a dented silver bowl; forgotten childhood artifacts that lend incongruous familiarity to this foreign space.

What do you think of the boys, he asks, of how they're doing? We are cycling along a canal, in a country as cute as a theme park. They're lovely, I say, but don't push them so hard; let flowers open up on their own. My eyes fill with tears. It is so much easier, I say, to see that you're doing a good job when they're small.

When it is time to go, he drives me to the train station. Let me buy your ticket, he says, thank you for making time to visit. Thank you for having me, I reply. Don't be a stranger. Twelve hours later, as I am driving home from the airport, he calls to make sure I'm okay.

11

Our big girl is home. She did well with tree planting, but seems to be falling back into depressive patterns, sleeping all day, watching movies and knitting all night, disengaging from family chores and games. My mum has a bad hip; the girls are going to weed her garden. I rouse the younger ones at 9:15 for a 10:00am departure but the eldest will not budge. This is not healthy, I say, and you know it. Let me manage my own life, she mumbles. After twenty minutes of futile discussion I lift her hips and slide her legs onto the floor. I love you enough to risk pissing you off, I say. In my house, you will get out of bed. Fine, she replies. I will find somewhere else to stay.

An hour later I come in from washing carpets and find her eating cereal. Amelia says I can stay at her house in the city, she says. I pause, considering. I think you're making a really poor choice, I reply, but clearly that's your choice to make. I go stare at my paper revisions, wondering what I should say if she asks for a ride to Amelia's.

That afternoon, I return from errands to find our big girl at the kitchen table. She comes in for a hug. Sorry, she says. She is much taller than me now. She wraps her arms around my shoulders. Her body is open and tender as a baby's. I'm sorry too, I say. I am still learning how to be the parent you need.

12

One Friday night I come in the back gate a few days after a windstorm. I notice in passing a black garbage bag caught in a tree. I glance at it again the next day. Sunday I open the upstairs back door to hang laundry and see that it is almost close enough to touch, but it is a bird, not a bag; a crow, wings spread, body twisted, caught in the branches. Terrible and beautiful—then it opens one round eye and looks at me. Oh my god I am so sorry bird I am so sorry bird I am so sorry. Sobbing. Hand over mouth. Oh my god oh my god oh my god. Shaking. Running back inside, bursting, going back to make sure it is real. The crow blinks and slowly flexes one claw. Fumbling for the phone, for my partner. Hi sweetie are you okay? No Shawnie there is a bird it is alive it is stuck in the tree it has been there for days I thought it was a plastic bag and poor bird I need you to help it I can't help it can you help it die?

A heavy pause. Okay, he says, I'm on my way. I wait with the bird. I want a photograph, to remember, to paint it, but I cannot bear to take its picture.

He arrives. I need you to help the bird right now, I say. He changes into scrubs, gets a hammer, an axe, a garbage bag. I cannot watch. After awhile he comes back in. How did it go? I ask, wringing my hands.

I got it out of the tree, he says. It was alive but its neck was broken. I put it on the ground and helped it die. It was, he adds, surprisingly full of yellow liquid; it burst like a water balloon. He takes off his clothes and gets in the shower.

I go out to the yard. Sorry bird, I say. Goodbye bird. I take two black feathers off the ground and put them someplace safe. Then I forget where they are.

Sophie Tamas
Department of Geography and Environmental Studies/
  School of Canadian Studies
Carleton University

DEREK M. BOLEN

AFTER DINNERS, IN THE GARAGE, OUT OF DOORS, AND CLIMBING ON ROCKS

Writing Aesthetic Moments of Father-Son

My brother Zack and I had recently been displaced from life—out of school, out of work, out of romantic relationships. Seeking respite, we began staying with our mom and dad in our childhood home. It didn't take much longer than a week of lazing around listening to sullen music and looping what we identified as key-childhood movies before our parents saw fit to tax the sanctuary we were taking with manual labor.

The hand-operated posthole auger mocks us—skipping and skidding about on the dark brown surface just below the green grass. The harder we push down on and rotate the auger, the closer the sun gets to us, and the warmer and muggier the day becomes. Sweat dripping from foreheads, dirt clinging to skin. With no lack of physical effort and a cacophonic polyphony of obscenities, we manage to finish one posthole. Standing a fence pole on end to admire our labor, we discover the hole isn't deep enough. An encore of all previously uttered obscenities erupts from my mouth just as dad rounds the corner of the garage.

"You shouldn't swear like that," dad responds. Although I wasn't aware that he'd hear me, I am caught off guard because numerous litmus tests that began upon high school graduation and escalated in frequency through college had confirmed that I could wield obscenities around my dad.

Unable to report on the findings of my rigorous longitudinal testing, and feeling vulnerable, I counter with, "You swear all the time."

Disappointed in the argument I've used, dad leaves little time for me to rehash my reasoning and says, "It's every father's hope for his son to be a better person than he was."

There's nothing for me to say in response. And I won't remember what happens next. I will remember this as a unique moment of closeness and connection—a moment unique among unique moments.

AESTHETIC MOMENTS

In Baxter's (2004, 2011) Bakhtinian dialogism-inspired articulation of relational dialectics 2.0, aesthetic moments (Bakhtin, 1990) "create momentary consummation, completion, or wholeness in what is otherwise a messy and fragmented life experience" (Baxter, 2004, p. 12). Aesthetic moments are relational experiences in/of/through communication. They represent peak experiences

J. Wyatt & T. E. Adams (eds.), On (Writing) Families, 141–147.

(Goodall & Kellett, 2004) of relating, in some ways resembling dialogic moments (Cissna & Anderson, 1998) as experiences of mutuality.

Baxter and DeGooyer (2001) characterized perceived aesthetic moments in conversation a number of ways, ranging from a completion of self through other, to present-focused relational closeness, to a cosmic oneness whereby relational members experience a connection together, to something outside of the relationship like nature. The communicative content of/in perceived aesthetic moments might also focus on the temporal continuity of the relationship it's experienced within— connecting present to future or past to present. The communication of perceived aesthetic moments may be characterized by an easy, natural conversational flow and/or deep, open talk. Although aesthetic moments are featured in Baxter's work, little else has been done.

Dialogically and relationally, aesthetic moments are intersubjectives. In autoethnographic narrative, aesthetic moments are subjectives akin to Baxter and DeGooyer's (2001) work with perceived aesthetic moments. I position aesthetic moments similar to epiphanies in that relational experience doesn't have to be verified by a relational other to be a perceived aesthetic experience. However, aesthetic moments are not all experiences to be subsumed by the influential *epiphany* moniker. Denzin's (1989) epiphany is often synonymous with life-altering crisis, strife, and the pursuant overcome. While some aesthetic moments are surely epiphanic, others are but one moment in a constellation of experience forming an epiphany. And then there are likely aesthetic moments that, for now, from this vantage point, appear as lone stars in the vastness of space. These aesthetic moments are mundane in their everyday, often overlooked because they lack transformative power. They may be oft forgotten until remembered and then forgotten again. In this essay, I offer a series of aesthetic moments to explore father-son communication and relationship.

Fourth Grade I's

We call them trips. Dad is gone for five or seven days at a time. They aren't sales trips or trips for training or conferences. They're camping trips. He's a wilderness instructor.

I spend my fourth grade days like all of the other fourth graders I know, building clay dioramas of scenes from *Charlotte's Web* (which look better in imaginations than in shoeboxes), dissecting giant grasshoppers, peering down microscopes, and itching to play *The Oregon Trail* on the Apple IIc at the back of the classroom. When I get home, mom makes dinner and we watch *Unsolved Mysteries* until it's time for bed. With dad out of town, I lock the back door before *Unsolved Mysteries* starts. When I forget, I dart across the dark house and flip the deadbolt as quickly as I can.

Even though dad is "unreachable" when he's on trips, I still know where I can find him—the garage. The garage is dad's space. When he's home, he works on projects in the garage. Woodworking projects, camping gear projects, remodelling projects. When he's on trips, if I miss him, I can go to the garage and look at his workbench with tools and gadgets that are for purposes I can only imagine (and always do). Even though he's gone, he's still here. When he's home, I go out to the garage with him. I have my own workbench in the back corner. When he's gone, I drag the garage stool, his stool, to my workbench and work on my garage projects. I am not supposed to be in the garage alone, so it doesn't take too long before mom calls out the back door for me to come back in the house. Then we watch *Unsolved Mysteries*. Sometimes with dinner, sometimes with popcorn after dinner, but always with the doors locked. And that's my job.

One chilly autumn night, I follow my dad to the garage after dinner. Under the full moon we see a stray cat with something hanging from its mouth. A closer look and the cat runs away. It drops what was in its mouth—a baby rabbit. His skin is torn, bloody. Chunks of fur are matted to a bright pink opening that reveals what lies just under flesh. I am sad, upset, scared. "We have to help him," I say. My dad scoops the shivering rabbit up in his hands and takes the bunny to his workbench. "Is he going to die?" I ask. "If we work fast, if you help me, we can try to help him," dad replies. "But it might not work," he warns. I ignore this part, nodding my head in commitment. The bunny is breathing heavy. His whole body throbs like my heart in my chest. The first aid kit is opened. Dad soaks some gauze with something from the paint cabinet.

"What's that for?" I ask.

"This should make him go to sleep so we can get a better look," he replies.

Wrapped in a clean white cloth, he looks...better. I hold him still. Dad holds the cloth to the rabbit's face. His face is small and cute and not bloody. But in his shiny eyes, I see fear. He settles down. My dad turns him over and draws back the white turned red cloth to reveal that half of his side is torn, tattered. His breaths are closer together, smaller. With antibiotic creams, bandages, needles, and thread at the ready, the baby rabbit's breathing slows and shallows. He stops moving. Although I don't want to, I hear dad say, "There was nothing we could do."

You and Me Both Care

Unlike report cards, which are delivered often and can be skillfully managed, my inaugural high school progress report made it clear that these reports were something like secrets sent across enemy lines. A form of teacher-parent espionage delivered to the mailbox hours before I would return home from school, progress reports were best marinated in my oblivion until being sprung after dinner.

Seemingly out of nowhere, a half sheet of paper from a carbon copy packet appears in my mom's hand just long enough to be passed to my dad. I recognize the paper to be something official ... from school. Dutifully performing the role of disaffected youth, I quickly steer the conversation to argument. Although my dad is often away, traveling for work, his absence is nothing compared to the emotional distance I design. I am an accomplished engineer of absenting others—particularly my dad. I believe they teach this in middle school, seventh or eighth grade. They slip it in between gym class and woodshop.

The conversation outlasts daylight because I can't understand why my dad doesn't understand. This becomes compounded for me by his apparent lack of understanding of why I can't understand. After what feels like hours of tactfully resisting reason, it's time for my consequences. I have to surrender my Sony Discman for an unspecified amount of time. I drag myself to my bedroom to retrieve my most valuable possession, taking my time. In my room, lamenting my collection of CDs, I recall Channel One's coverage of the separation of church and state debate and begin to consider the merits of a separation of home and school. But then I remember that my dad is to blame for this. On my brief walk back, I fail to come up with anything new to say.

With the cord of the headphones wound neatly around my Discman, I silently slide it across the table. Picking up from the table with my teenage life in his hands, he says, "I am doing this because I care." I find my final dig, "Was Hallmark out of cards? Most people just send cards to say they care." As he's walking out of the kitchen, he laughs at what I've said. Careful to hide it, I laugh at him laughing. A few hours later, rolling over in bed, I close my eyes and replay him laughing at what I said. I realize that he did understand why I wasn't understanding, that I did understand why he wasn't understanding.

Finding Each Other

I usually frame my coming out story as nothing spectacular, generally devoid of narrative merit. When I was 23, my mom came over for a visit and insisted on putting my clean clothes away.

I turn my back for a few minutes, and she's finding places for the clothes she's folded using the context clues of what she sees in the drawers. From a drawer filled with winter socks she pulls out a rainbow flag, which I had partially folded and shoved into the back. After a supportive, albeit awkward talk, we decide I should be the one to tell my dad. Already late getting picked up by my boyfriend to go to Cedar Point, the closest major amusement park, I decide to postpone talking with my dad. The next day, when I don't answer my phone or my door, with my car still in my driveway, she becomes worried and tells my dad everything. I return her call later that evening after a day of riding rollercoasters. I learn that she's told my dad. Although much repair has been done to close the distance created in my teenage years, my reaction is to avoid my dad for months.

More than anything, the passing of time increases my anxiety. When I finally make the two-hour trip to go home, I don't bring it up. I decide the topic is still too fresh, too raw to simply be brought up. But I know that I need to talk with my dad. I know that my avoidance is running in the same vein as the distancing from my teenage years. We eat dinner. Things feel more settled. Life here at home, it's gone on even after finding out that I am gay. After dinner, my dad makes his way to the garage. I follow. Opening the backdoor, I see the glowing translucent fiberglass garage door. I step out of the house and walk toward the garage.

In the middle of the garage floor is a large gaming table setup for my younger brother. My dad sits on a stool on one side. I sit on a stool across from him. We

144

start to talk. First about college—I am about to graduate and begin graduate school. I guide the conversation. He lets me. Eventually, I find my way to talking about sexuality ... and then to talking about my sexuality. He doesn't rush me, he doesn't stop me, and he doesn't prompt me. Now that I am finally here, I begin asking him questions. I hadn't planned on asking him questions. But I ask him about his faith. He's Catholic. I'm not. We talk through religion and spirituality. The talk comes easy. My worries that one of us will say something incommensurable with the other's beliefs, with the other's being, quickly fade. I ask him questions about cultural and social issues concerning sexuality. For the first time, he begins to ask me questions. He inquires into my relationship. He inquires into my well-being. He inquires into my being. When we finish talking, telling stories that too often seem to have a way of making distance and fostering absence, I feel closer to him than I ever have. The next day I drive back to school. I wonder what I was so worried about. I wonder why I waited. I decide that times like this, they're worth not having answers.

CODA

For me, father-son exists between the two words. That small mark is the space for communication, relating, and experience. In this essay, I have offered a series of aesthetic moments of father-son—moments in which my father and I, to borrow from Pelias (2011), leaned in and toward each other. They're stories where—despite obstacles of life, relating, and cultural imperatives—closeness, openness, connection, and mutuality were achieved, if only for a moment. Aesthetic moments are, by virtue, wholly good moments—some through a few words, some through conversations, some through doing, and some only through hindsight.

A Final Moment

Bochner's (1997) essay on career, narrative, and the death of his father resonates with me—partly as a cautionary tale. I don't want to write my family out of my life story, but the commitment made to an academic life often has a way of doing this anyway. When my dad invites me to go rock climbing with him and my brother at the end of my final semester of doctoral coursework, I am excited to have the time and be able to go.

We drive ten hours to Devil's Lake, a state park in Wisconsin. We set up camp as the sun goes down. I shiver in my tent with Raider, my dog. Zack and dad are in a tent next to me talking quietly, planning tomorrow's climbs. I know that Zack and dad have more experiences camping together than I do. I try not to think about it.

We wake to pack our daypacks with food, water, and climbing gear. I bring my iPad. As dad and Zack ready the first climb, I settle in atop the rock face. I sit this climb out to write a book chapter. About half finished with my writing, they finish the first climb and we move on to another. I feel here, but not really. My only climb of the day is a search for cell service to send off my chapter. By the time I finish, the setting sun ends the last climb. Back at camp, we eat dinner. I am proud of what I've written but resent the time that it has taken me away from them. A cold night, shivering in my sleeping bag with Raider. Tomorrow it rains, so we'll go into town. The next day, we'll climb.

Daypacks packed, sans iPad. Dad and Zack comb through the climbing maps. Zack climbs first. I watch to remember how it's done. Dad belays.

"On belay," Zack says at the bottom of the rock.

"Belay on," dad replies.

"Climbing," Zack follows.

"Climb on," dad responds.

A rope from the belayer runs to the top of the climb, comes back down, and is hooked to the climber's harness. The commands are for safety. When the belay is on, the belayer takes up the slack created by the climber's ascent. Because the belayer has a different vantage point, s/he can offer the climber advice. Zack makes it to the top and lowers down. My turn.

The harness clings and pulls in all of the wrong places. I am nervous. Not of falling or getting hurt, but nervous that I won't be able to do this. Waiting for my turn, I remembered that the last time I had climbed was in high school. I watched everyone else climb, feigning disinterest. In many ways, at 30, this is my first time.

"On belay," I say at the bottom of the rock.

"Belay on," dad replies.

"Climbing," I follow.

"Climb on," dad responds.

My slow climb starts. It's a struggle, harder than I thought it would be. The higher I get, the more I want to come down. Face to face with uneven rock, I reach my hand above me. Feeling around for a hold, a groove in or protrusion of the rock where I can take grip. Below me my feet are out of sight. I get stuck, but feel safe with dad belaying. I am climbing with my dad.

"Sometimes your best next move is below you, sometimes you need to go back," dad offers.

I understand what he means, but I can't see how it will help me. Not even halfway up the rock face, feeling as though there's no place to go, I am ready to come down.

"I think I am ready to come down."

"Are you sure?" dad asks.

"Yeah. Ready to lower," I say.

"Lowering," dad responds.

Lowering through the air, the face of the rock passes by my own. It doesn't seem as hard, as difficult. I think about what I've just given up.

"Off belay," I say, feet on ground.

"Belay off," dad replies.

Perhaps he has always been belaying me, clipping me on and off as needed.

While unhooking my ropes and removing my harness, dad and Zack both congratulate me on a good climb, "Nice work up there!" In this adventure of relating through doing, I am with my dad.

Zack clips in to belay dad. While dad climbs, I think about everything that I've missed out on. Missed out on from distancing myself growing up. Missed out on from not opening up. Missed out on from choosing school. At 55-years-old, he effortlessly moves past the spot where I struggled—the spot where I stopped. He makes moves forward and upward. And, at times, thoughtfully makes moves backward and downward. When he reaches the top, I wonder how many years I'll have left with him. I wonder how many more times I'll make choices that create distance and absence in our relationship. I hope not many.

Sometimes your best move is back.

REFERENCES

Bakhtin, M. M. (1990). *Art and answerability* (M. Holquist, Ed.; V. Liapunov & K. Brostrom, Trans.). Austin: University of Texas Press.

Baxter, L. A. (2004). Relationships as dialogues. *Personal Relationships, 11*, 1-22.

Baxter, L. A. (2011). *Voicing relationships: A dialogic perspective.* Thousand Oaks, CA: Sage.

Baxter, L. A., & DeGooyer, D. H., Jr. (2001). Perceived aesthetic characteristics of interpersonal conversations. *Southern Communication Journal, 67*(1), 1-18.

Bochner, A. P. (1997). It's about time: Narrative and the divided self. *Qualitative Inquiry, 3*, 418-438.

Cissna, K. N., & Anderson, R. (1998). Theorizing about dialogic moments: The Buber-Rogers position and postmodern themes. *Communication Theory, 8*, 63-104.

Denzin, N. K. (1989). *Interpretive interactionism.* Newbury Park, CA: Sage.

Goodall, H. L., & Kellett, P. M. (2004). Dialectical tensions and dialogic moments as pathways to peak experiences. In R. Anderson, L. A. Baxter, & K. N. Cissna (Eds.), *Dialogue: Theorizing difference in communication studies* (pp. 159-174). Thousand Oaks, CA: Sage.

Pelias, R. (2011). *Leaning: A poetics of personal relations.* Walnut Creek, CA: Left Coast Press.

Derek M. Bolen
Department of Communication and Mass Media
Angelo State University

TONY E. ADAMS AND JONATHAN WYATT

TIES THAT BIND, TIES THAT SCAR

I (Tony) have many scars from living in Danville, Illinois (United States), a factory and farming town of about 30,000 people in which I spent the first twenty years of my life. I have scars of the community's conservatism, misogyny, racism, and poverty; scars of secret adoptions and belittled mental illnesses; and scars of heteronormative expectations, unnerving silences, and distanced and abandoned family. I try to do my best to ignore or camouflage these scars, though I have found this process to be difficult, if not impossible.

I suppose that my parents had grand desires for me. I suppose that they tried their best to insulate me from the harms of Danville, always wanting to make my life the best that it could be. They encouraged me to get a college education, and they supported me when I left the rural and repressive community to seek better personal and professional opportunities. But in some ways their encouragement and support for my education and my need to leave now haunts me/us—they're still in Danville, and I'm not; I don't like to visit and I never want to (permanently) return. And, as I write this, I suppose that I have a new scar, one of worrying—believing—that I no longer have much in common with them.

Or maybe I do: I am most content when I work and the happiest when I write. I wake up most everyday looking for the next task. Some folks think that I'm weird, and they worry about my heath and exhaustion: I'm teaching too many classes, they say, working with too many students, writing too much, serving on too many committees. But when I return to Danville, I rarely see my mother stopping to rest: there are always dishes to wash, cats to feed, carpets to vacuum, cabinets in need of paint, gutters clogged with leaves, and organizations in need of volunteers. I see my father operating his restaurant every day and night, rarely being able to take a break from the business. And on a recent visit to his house, I watched him vigilantly mop the floor, scrub the walls, and rearrange the furniture. I recognize that he is tired from his work and in pain from another kidney stone, but he says that he cannot rest—he likes to work and there's much more work to do. My mother and father don't stop moving; in some ways I have become them.

I also suppose that my parents taught me to never think that I am better, higher, more enlightened than anyone else. With students, I refuse to be called "Doctor" and instead ask to be referred to as "Tony." I wear hats, shorts, slippers, and sometimes sandals to class and I often meet off-campus with students. I am not better, higher, more enlightened than them; they are humans, wanting, trying, struggling to make it day-by-day, just like me. While I might have more experience reading and writing about particular topics, I do not feel that my "knowledge"

J. Wyatt & T. E. Adams (eds.), On (Writing) Families, 149–150.

trumps their "knowledge." Instead, and by example, my parents taught me to listen to—and not talk at—others, to see what I can learn from them.

And I suppose that my ability to take life seriously but also not too serious, stemmed from my parents as well. My mom is frequently irreverent and my father likes to joke. The three of us poke fun at the most dire of circumstances, knowing that today might be our last day together—one of us could die now, or in a few hours, or later this week—and we do our best to enjoy *and* recognize our limited and passing time. (For instance, when people ask me "How are you?" I often reply, like my mother, with "I'm fine. I woke up today.") Like my parents, I too am often irreverent because, in my limited life-time, I like to laugh. I recognize that such a cheeky-ability is quite privileged—there is much harm in the world—but everyday I pledge to be the best person possible, to attend to and care for others, and to do my best to correct social wrongs while, simultaneously, appreciate my ability to breath, think, move.

*

The contributors to this collection make me think about the statement, "wherever you go, there you are": I am my past, my parents, Danville. No matter how far I run and no matter how frequently we talk or visit, I am still my family—in speech and grammar, kindness and ignorance, mannerisms and eating habits, morals and expectations. My family ties—some adoptive, some biological, some chosen—inform my past, present, and future desires, plans, and abilities; they are ties that bind and scar wherever I go, ties replete with presence and absence, love and loss.

*

The experience of my family changes every day. We age and fall ill. We experience joy and happiness, sorrow and tragedy, and joy and happiness again. We abandon and create allegiances, make and reveal secrets, eliminate and establish rules and boundaries. We scar and get scarred by each other, inflicting and tending to wounds that may never heal.

Tony E. Adams
Department of Communication, Media and Theatre
Northeastern Illinois University

Jonathan Wyatt
Counselling and Psychotherapy
The University of Edinburgh

Lightning Source UK Ltd.
Milton Keynes UK
UKOW05f0626090517
300805UK00009B/717/P